HUMAN FREEDOM AND SOCIAL ORDER

HUMAN FREEDOM AND SOCIAL
ORDER / *An Essay in Christian Philosophy*

John Wild

Harvard University

PUBLISHED FOR THE LILLY ENDOWMENT RESEARCH
PROGRAM IN CHRISTIANITY AND POLITICS BY THE
DUKE UNIVERSITY PRESS, DURHAM, N. C.   1959

Printed in the United States of America

Foreword

It is a curious fact that the Age of Reason ushered in so confidently by the *philosophes* of the eighteenth century has given way in the twentieth century to an Age of Anxiety. The extension of reason through science and technology, the ever-increasing mastery of the human environment, while it has led to unprecedented human power on the one hand, has led on the other to the diminution of individual freedom and human dignity. A distinguished professor of philosophy at Harvard University, John Wild, addresses himself to this phenomenon in the pages that follow and examines the universal experience of anxiety in the light of a Christian understanding of the meaning of human existence and freedom. More particularly he asks: Is a Christian philosophy possible? And how can we bridge the chasm that separates politics from Christian ethics?

The present volume is based upon a series of three lectures which Professor Wild delivered at Duke University in November, 1958 under the auspices of the Lilly Endowment Research Program in Christianity and Politics. The ideas expressed here, of course, are those of the author and do not necessarily reflect those of the Research Program nor of Lilly Endowment, Inc.

The Research Program in Christianity and Politics was inaugurated at Duke University in the fall of 1957 by a generous grant from Lilly Endowment. One feature of the program is an annual series of public lectures by a distinguished scholar who has an interest in bringing his Christian concerns to bear upon the problems of politics and the social order.

These lectures, as well as occasional monographs, will be published by the Duke University Press.

It is appropriate that the first volume in this series should address itself to the question whether a Christian philosophy is possible and that it should be written by a man eminently qualified to undertake such an inquiry. John Wild received both the Ph.B. degree and the Ph.D. degree from the University of Chicago. He has been teaching in the philosophy department of Harvard University since 1927 and has also been associated with the faculty of the Harvard Divinity School since 1954. His numerous writings include: *Plato's Theory of Man* (1946), *Introduction to Realistic Philosophy* (1948), *Plato's Modern Enemies and the Theory of Natural Law* (1953), and *The Challenge of Existentialism* (1955).

John H. Hallowell, *Director*

*Lilly Endowment Research Program
in Christianity and Politics*

Advisory Committee:

Waldo Beach
Professor of Christian Ethics, Duke Divinity School

Ralph J. D. Braibanti
Professor of Political Science, Duke University

Robert E. Cushman
Dean of the Duke Divinity School

Alan K. Manchester
Dean of Trinity College, Duke University

H. Shelton Smith
Professor of American Religious Thought, Duke Divinity School

Robert R. Wilson
Professor of Political Science, Duke University

Preface

In other parts of the world, philosophy is recognized as a basic human need to be fulfilled, so far as this is possible, through the acts of living men inspired by religious ideals and images that have been developed in the histories of different lands. Thus we speak naturally of a Buddhist philosophy, a Hindu philosophy, and a Confucian philosophy, and in our own tradition we distinguish between English, French, German, and Marxist philosophies. But until very recently the term *Christian Philosophy* has not been received into common usage, and it is now clear that this is no mere verbal accident. It is rather the expression of a noteworthy gap in our intellectual history.

The possibility of a Christian philosophy has been glimpsed by a few original thinkers like Augustine, Pascal, and Kierkegaard but it has never been coherently and persistently worked out as an independent discipline. Instead of this, Christian faith has been combined with an abstract mode of objectivist thought which arose in Greece under the inspiration of alien religious sources. This type of philosophy claims to have access to a divine faculty of reason in man which is able to apprehend the timeless essences of all things, and to deduce a closed system of being from self-evident principles. In the course of our history, these conceptions have been subjected to a very searching criticism, partly coming from Christian sources, which in our time has had its effect. Many of our contemporaries find it hard to believe in a worldless faculty of reason separate from the rest of human nature. They doubt whether any closed system will ever be finally demonstrated in such a way as to rule out all other alternatives and thus to end our intellectual history.

Hence the idea of an open Christian philosophy striving as a purely human discipline to take account of the evidence accessible to all, but ultimately inspired by the guiding image of Christian faith has now emerged as a living option for the more chastened and self-critical thought of our time. The present work is devoted to an exploration of this possibility. In Part One we shall examine its general nature and the objections that may be urged against it. In Part Two we shall try to work it out in certain areas of social and political philosophy which are still largely untouched by Christian existential thinking.

Chapters IV, V, and VI are based on the Walter Freeman Whitman Lectures, entitled *"Christian Thought and the World of Today,"* delivered at Nashotah House in May, 1958, and I am grateful to Dean White for his permission to publish some of this material in its present form. Certain parts of Chapters I, II, and VIII were delivered as the Lilly Foundation Lectures on Christianity and Politics at Duke University in November, 1958. The present volume is in fact a reformulation and development of these lectures.

I wish to express my thanks to Professor Calvin Schrag of Purdue University and to Professor Geoffrey Clive of Clark University for their reading and helpful criticism of the manuscript. I am also grateful to the Joseph H. Clark Bequest of Harvard University for a grant which enabled me to prepare the text for publication.

J. W.

Cambridge, Mass.
July 1959

Table of Contents

Part Two

CHRISTIAN ETHICS AND SOCIAL PHILOSOPHY

Chapter Five

THE METHOD AND CONTENT OF CHRISTIAN PHILOSOPHY

127

Chapter Six

CHRISTIAN ETHICS

153

Part One

CHRISTIAN THOUGHT
AND GNOSTICISM

Chapter One

MYTHICAL LIFE AND THE
GNOSTIC ENTERPRISE

This volume is devoted to the exploration of a new possibility now opening up before us—the idea of a Christian philosophy. By this we mean not the irresponsible formulation of a private or sectarian view of the world untested by evidence available to all, but a free and autonomous discipline subject to empirical check and yet looking, where ultimate decisions are involved, toward a Christian guiding image. Every human philosopher faces such ultimate decisions and, unless his procedure is to become purely arbitrary, he must follow a guiding image of some kind. Hence the Christian philosopher is by no means peculiar in this respect. He takes the same risks as other philosophers, is subject to the same disappointments, and is responsible to the same evidence. But where this evidence is ambiguous, as it often is at basic levels, he looks to a Christian guiding image.

In a penetrating and well-known article published in 1931 [1] Émile Bréhier, the French historian of philosophy, after a careful examination of the claims that can be made for Augustine, Aquinas, Descartes, Hegel, and others, concluded that a Christian philosophy of this sort has never yet been formulated. In this article I believe that Bréhier has somewhat overstated his case, and that exceptions must be made for certain aspects at least of Augustinian thought,

[1] "Y a-t-il une philosophie chretienne?", *Revue de Métaphysique et de Morale*, XXXVIII (1931), 133 ff.

and for certain antitraditional critics like Pascal and Kierkegaard. But aside from rare exceptions of this kind, I believe
that his conclusion is essentially correct. The rationalist
tradition of detached, objective thought, which has dominated our intellectual history, came originally from ancient
Greece, where it was inspired by non-Christian images and
feelings. Certain of its later manifestations were combined
with special versions of Christian faith. But such combina-
tions left the basic structures of objective reason intact. The
result was not so much a tradition of philosophy internally
moved by a Christian image as an array of rational systems,
each claimed by its supporters to be compatible with
Christian faith.

In the absence of any living tension between the two, it
is not surprising that reason has often pressed its claims
beyond their proper limits. Impelled by its own sense of
logical rigor and self-sufficiency, it has presented the world
with vast, inclusive systems pretending not only to reveal
the cosmic order in which we exist but to calculate our way
to self-realization and happiness. It cannot be denied that
faith also has often overstepped its limits and tried to do
the work of philosophy. But, taking our history as a whole,
it is not so much reason and science that have been fideized
as faith that has been rationalized. Thus Augustine gave
way to Aquinas in the end, and Kant gave way to Hegel.
But this conquest of abstract objectivity and certainty over
concrete subjectivity and uncertainty has not been able to
escape from a vigorous protest and criticism that has persisted through our history. This protest began with Paul's
attack on the foolish pretensions of worldly philosophy (I
Cor. 3:19), which has been continued by a living tradition
of preaching down to the present time, and which found
philosophical expression in the works of critics like Pascal
and Kierkegaard. Greek philosophy was merged with its
own special form of religiosity that has haunted the works

of reason ever since. But the Pauline criticism has had its effect in the end. This factor more than any other has brought about that secularization of philosophy which we have at last achieved.

As reason has been gradually deflated and thoroughly humanized, faith has been increasingly derationalized, so that we can at last regard them independently apart from mutual intermixture and contamination. At the same time, when regarded in this way, the imperfection and dependence of each of them becomes quite evident. Why then should they not be brought into a living, dialectical tension with each other? Why should this tension not prove fruitful without any real confusion of the two, but with each retaining its integrity intact? Why not a Christian philosophy that is both an authentic philosophy and at the same time genuinely Christian? It is this possibility, now recognized by Catholics as well as Protestants,[2] that we are about to explore in the following pages.

We shall divide them into eight chapters consisting of two parts of four chapters each. Owing to the general unfamiliarity of the subject we shall devote Part One (Chapters I–IV) to a preparatory study of the nature of the project, comparing it and contrasting it with what has gone before, and answering major objections that will be raised. In Chapter I we shall try to gain a clearer conception of traditional rationalism by examining its origin from the "primitive" world of myth which marks the beginning of our cultural history. In Chapter II we shall try to show how religion remains, even after the passing of myth, as an unavoidable dimension of the human life-world. We shall also suggest an interpretation of Christian faith which, though only a

---

[2] E. Gilson, *The Christian Philosophy of St. Thomas Aquinas* (London: Gollancz, 1957); I. Trethowan, *An Essay in Christian Philosophy* (London: Longmans, 1954); and L. Hodgson, *Toward a Christian Philosophy* (London: Nisbet, 1946). Many other works could be cited in this connection, but these titles are sufficient to indicate the current trend I have in mind.

brief sketch, is sufficient in our opinion to show its radical difference from both mythical thought and rationalism. The third chapter will be devoted to a critical study of the problem of faith and reason which has plagued the history of Christian thought, and of the major "solutions" so far proposed. In Chapter IV we shall consider basic objections to the whole enterprise of a Christian philosophy. This will conclude Part One.

Having thus prepared the way by this introduction, we shall devote Part Two primarily to an exploration of certain definite themes of Christian ethics and social philosophy. In Chapter V we shall deal with the method and major divisions of this discipline, paying special attention to one of these, the revealing of the human life-world, then in Chapter VI with Christian ethics. In Chapter VII we shall be concerned with the clarification of certain basic concepts of social philosophy, such as community, civilization, and culture, and with the notorious chasm which now separates Christianity from politics. Finally in Chapter VIII we shall examine the relation between the human person and the group, and ways of bridging the chasm. This will conclude the present volume.

Through the whole of our study, we shall be constantly concerned with the human *Lebenswelt,* first opened up for disciplined study under Christian inspiration in the thought of Kierkegaard. It is this exploration and partial illumination of the *Lebenswelt* that has reoriented the living thought of our time and confronted it with new possibilities beyond traditional rationalism. If we are now to explore one of these and to break with this tradition, it will be most important for us, first of all, to clarify our understanding of what we are departing from. What are the basic attitudes and conceptions of rationalist thought? In order to answer this question, we shall now compare it with the world of myth from which it emerged at the beginning of our cultural history.

1. From Myth to Reason: The Origin of Western History

We shall have no time, of course, for any detailed outline of our Western history. We must be highly selective, and in this effort to focus what is essential, we shall call the reader's attention to a major transition which lies at the origin of our Western history, and which has recently been illumined by several important studies in anthropology and phenomenology.[3] This is the transition from a mythical to a rational mode of existence which occurred long ago in our history in the islands of Ionia and in ancient Greece, but which has now been studied at first hand in the case of certain existing, so-called primitive cultures. We shall try briefly to clarify these two ways of life, and the nature of this transition which lies at the beginning of our history. Then we shall turn to a persistent problem it has left which remains to the present day.

The plant and even the animal, to a lesser degree, are at one with their environment. They are simply what they are. Their possibilities are narrowly restricted to modes of response determined by their structure, and they are unable to gain any distance from their surroundings to question the sense of what they do. But when man appears on the scene, this unity is broken. Man transcends himself. His existence divides into a manifold of possibilities which always project him beyond himself, and make him more than what he is. This transcendence gives him a certain distance from his factual condition, and leads him to question himself,

[3] See G. Van der Leeuw, *L'Homme primitif et la religion* (Paris: Alcan, 1940); M. Eliade, *Traité d'histoire des religions* (Paris: Payot, 1953); and G. Gusdorf, *Mythe et métaphysique* (Paris: Flammarion, 1953).

indeed to bring all things into question, and to ask for their sense.

Myth is the first answer to these questions, the sense that man bestows on his world as it comes into being, in his first attempt to recapture a lost unity before the anxiety, suffering, and death that belong to his existence. It is not a first product of understanding, nor a primitive kind of reason. It is rather the structure of an initial mode of awareness quite distinct from any form of reason. In order to grasp this difference, which is now hard to convey succinctly in our rationalized language, let us now turn to myth as it is found in primitive cultures still living, and summarize its most distinctive features, paying special attention to the account of a New Guinea tribe which is presented by Maurice Leenhardt in his book *Do Kamo*.

Mythical understanding is active and incarnate in the world—not detached. Thus in the Melanesian language described by Leenhardt, the word NO may be translated by *word,* but not in such a way as to exclude the object of a discourse.[4] The word is the revealing of act, object, and meaning, all three. Thus a gift offering is a word. For every family ceremonial, a little pile of edible objects is prepared and carefully placed on the ritual herbs. When all is ready, the family assembles in a semicircle and the orator says: *These are our word.* The act itself and its object bear a message. There may also be a discourse in support of the gift. But this is another gift, not an offering but an homage. The word is joined to the act it expresses, but the act is more essential.

Man and the world are directly lived and felt as one. A mountain, for example, is experienced as participating in life. This direct grasp of the world is often interpreted as a kind of primitive animism similar to what we suppose to be the attitude of a child who kicks the rock on which he has stubbed his toe. But this is an intellectualistic simpli-

[4] M. Leenhardt, *Do Kamo* (Paris: Gallimard, 1947), p. 166.

fication. The primitive has no view of an inanimate nature which is then personified. Our language refers to the foot, the flanks, the shoulder, the neck, and the face of a mountain, and we speak of these as metaphorical modes of speech. But for the primitive, it is no metaphor to think of the mountain as a rough and stormy giant. These terms express the resistance of the mountain as it is lived, a certain way of being in the world.

The primitive man is not detached from these objects of his lived experience. He is with them in his world. Thus the surrounding beings with which he lives are not neutral objects. The river, the tree, and the mountain are *his*. Hence he can participate and join with them. Such participation is a prominent and noteworthy factor in primitive thought.[5] Through the myth, it has created and ordered a world of its own in which it is at home. With the things it has ordered in this way it can identify itself. Culture and nature are not separated. Man and his world are one.

At the heart of the myth is the sacred, or the divine, a power transcending man and the whole human world. This creative power manifests itself in certain objects, particularly those which are unusual and strange. Thus in the Celebes when the fruit of a banana tree grows not from the top but from the middle of the trunk, this is *measa,* and ordinarily leads to the death of the master of the tree.[6] An enormous tree or a great storm may be the temporary dwelling place of the divine. The wind lashing the lagoon into a fury of waves is said to be God walking on the waters. The Shilluks in the Sudan apply the name of the Supreme Being, which is *Juok,* to anything monstrous and extraordinary, to anything, in fact, which a Shilluk cannot understand.[7] But the object itself need not be novel or strange. It

[5] Cf. G. Van der Leeuw, *Phänomenologie der Religion* (2d ed.; Tübingen: J. C. B. Mohr, 1956).
[6] Eliade, *op. cit.,* p. 26.
[7] *Ibid.,* p. 36.

suffices that it be connected with crucial experiences such as birth, sickness, and death, or that it be fitted into a pattern symbolizing the transcendent. There is, in fact, no important object of human experience which has not served to incarnate (reveal) the transcendent which is over all, and, therefore, capable of being manifested by anything. But since it is always other than such a thing, no symbol is ever sufficient. Hence the vast diversity of primitive symbols, and the inner dialectic with which every historic religion has constantly been involved.

This mythical transcendence is characterized by an indeterminate indifference often symbolized by night. It is above all the contrarieties and quarrels which arise from the determinate traits of things and persons in the world. Thus, as we have seen, the mythical divinity is both sweet and terrible, creative and destructive, lord over life and death, hidden as well as revealed. In a way that is far more poignant than any rational discourse, the myth reveals to us a transcendent coincidence of opposites beyond all determinate attributes and antagonisms. In the phenomenon of the orgy and the orgiastic rite, we are presented with a rudimentary attempt of the religious life to attain a condition which is indistinct, and where all determinate experiences are abolished in a unity of opposites. This idea is also expressed in the myths of bisexual divinity, which are extremely widespread. The intention of such myths is to convey a sense of cosmic reintegration in a divine being which is perfect and complete, and beyond all partiality and antagonism. This being is, therefore, the source of all existence and value, a moving horizon of ultimate meaning never to be encompassed or exhaustively possessed.

Hence the many literary myths of those hard and distant voyages over stormy seas, through narrow rockbound passages and dangers of every kind, which symbolize the search of man for the divine. These are only vestiges of earlier initiation ceremonies where the voyage is acted out and expressed in a living liturgy. The end is inexhaustible and beyond us. Nevertheless it can be approached and entered, to some degree gained and revealed here and now. It is through such an initiation that the primitive gains a sense of his world as a whole, the union of sun and moon and all other opposites. In the light of this transcendence he can now find his own place and the place of everything with which he is concerned. From this time on, the sacred rites are the center of his life and that of the whole community whose common existence becomes a constantly repeated liturgy.

The myth expressed in these rites is a model which has often taken the form of an account of the original creation of the world after which all sound action and any making of anything must be patterned. Thus according to a Polynesian myth, *Ta' aroa,* who brought forth all the Gods and who created the whole world, has lived from all eternity within a shell that is like an egg rolling forever through unlimited space.[8] The egg here symbolizes the constant renewal of life, like the flowering of vegetation in the spring, which is a repetition of the original act of creation. This symbol of the cosmogonic egg is found not only in our so-called Easter eggs but in ancient India, Persia, Greece, Phœnicia, Esthonia, Finland, West Africa, Central and South America. It signifies the first creation of the entire world spelled out in different ways by the myths of different peoples. In this original creation, every person and thing found its archetypal place in its archetypal form. In the rites of many peoples this creation is acted out in such a way that the whole life of the community is a constant renewal and repetition of this archetypal act in the great time of the beginning of all things. This myth gives meaning to every object in the world and persists through the flux of time.

[8] *Ibid.,* p. 353.

But the space and time of this primordial world are quite different from the rational and scientific meanings of these terms. There is no unlimited geographic space, but only the life-space lying around them which is occupied by the objects of their care. It is not everywhere the same but divided into different levels which are qualitatively different, like the subterranean, the earthly, and superior heavenly zones of the world of the Solomon Islanders. All three meet at the post of the dwelling house which plunges into the lower zone, and the top of which touches the heaven. Roundabout are the places of objects of care, the region of fishing, the region of planting, and the central place of the sacred symbols. Beyond this life space which belongs to them, there are strange worlds belonging to others, like the island of the dead and the ports to which the steamboats sail. But *their* space ends with the things they actually experience in the life of their daily cares. They carry it with them if the tribe has to move. This is *their* world, and beyond it lies a nothing-with-which-they-have-to-do.[9]

Their time is similarly limited, and divided into durations that are qualitatively distinct. But these durations are grasped as acts of a certain kind rather than as periods of time. Time and human existence are not distinguished. The motions of the sun and the phases of the moon are noted, and used to mark off different times—the time of the peach, the time of fishing, hunting, etc. There are no clocks and, therefore, no moments and dates. What we call time is measured by action, as the time required for the burning of a torch— before one must light another. Careful study of the language as spoken shows that while movement toward the future and the past can be noted, what we call the future and the past are really lacking.[10] The speaker in remembering a "past" event is not only *at* his own time but also at the time

---

[9] Leenhardt, *op. cit.*, pp. 61–66.
[10] *Ibid.*, pp. 97 ff.

of which he is speaking. They are two strands of existence marked by different qualities that are lived together. Hence there is no such thing as history. In the view of these Melanesians, there is no historic succession, but rather a series of levels that are superimposed and pushing each other into the night. Back of all this is the great time of the creative myth which is constantly repeated and renewed—a long time, and another long time, as the natives say.

Leenhardt has also shown that the individual fails to identify himself with his own individual body.[11] His self is taken up by the group. He *is* the social role that he plays from day to day. But on exceptional occasions, he can also adopt other roles with the aid of a mask. He constantly lives his identity with his totem, and has no difficulty in transporting himself into the totemic domain. In speaking of the totem, his presence and that of the totem exist simultaneously on two parallel planes. He has no definite sense of his own body, which merges with other physical things surrounding it. He is the various roles that he plays in the mythical life of the tribe which repeats the heroic existence of that great time. He is a *personage,* not a person inhabiting an individual body, and capable of a history.

Such is the mythical existence of primitive man as it is now being revealed to us by the epoch-making investigations of anthropologists and phenomenologists of our time. This is the first world established by man before the beginning of history. The facts that it has survived in certain primitive cultures still existing, and that it has left permanent traces in all historic civilizations strongly indicate to us that it contains moments of lasting significance.

This mythical consciousness is not separated from itself or from the objects of its concern. It is immediately joined to its own acts, and participates in these objects. A felt apprehension of mystery transcending all the specific at-

[11] *Ibid.,* chap. xi.

tributes and oppositions of things-in-the-world lies at its very heart and gives unity to its world. All human acts and all their objects are ordered to this transcendent and creative mystery. The different regions of care are never separated from each other, but constantly grasped together in global feelings like awe, anxiety, and joy which pervade and saturate every mythical mode of awareness.

The production of material goods, the care for health, and the education of the young all have their place in the same mythical context, and are pervaded by what we call religious meaning. In time of stress, the authority of the medicine man extends to all of them. Politics also belongs to religion. The chief has no special insignia nor authority of his own.[12] He simply represents the myth and exercises the functions that it assigns. Each personage of the tribe is identified in some way with this myth and simply repeats it as it is renewed with the liturgy of each generation.[13]

This world gives a stable human answer to the chaos, sickness, anxiety, and death which constantly threaten human existence. There are elements of permanent value in this answer. But as we examine it with some care, we are also aware of defects. This world is narrow and restricted to the immediate life-space of the tribe. It suppresses the dimension of time; it is fixed and frozen. No problems of meaning ever disturb its rigid immobility. There are no persons living their own individual bodies. Even this human body is an instrument for the tribal myth. These personages are not persons. They are covered by the masks that constitute their social roles.

As a result of this, there are no individual events to make up a human history. So as we look back to this mythical life we find that it has no time of its own. We have to allot it a kind of time which belongs to our world, and which

[12] *Ibid.*, pp. 141–146.
[13] Cf. Eliade, *op. cit.*, chap. xi; and Leenhardt, *op. cit.*, pp. 201–210.

things in the world only *have,* as a mineral *has* an age, as
we say. This mythical life is hard and congealed like a
rock. So in classifying its various divisions, and in allotting
to them their periods in world time, we use hard, impersonal categories, referring to them as the stone age, the bronze
age, the iron age, etc. These palaeolithic and neolithic
cultures seem rather to belong to the ages of geology than
to the periods of a human history.

This brief sketch will perhaps suggest some of the reasons
why we now understand the transition from a mythical to
a rational mode of awareness which occurred in ancient
Greece as a critical, perhaps the most critical, step in our
Western history. It is this rational mode of thought and
existence which has governed our life since that time. Of
this we must now attempt to give a broad and general
sketch.

2. *Rational Thought and Existence*

Since we are now to consider a basic and constant trend
in our culture with which we are all familiar, we must be
content with a much briefer outline. Certain general features
of the change from mythical to rational life, which occurred
at the beginning of Greek history, are well known. Contradictions are found in the traditional myths which call forth
individual reflection of an objective kind. Men not only
live these myths; they think about them from a detached
point of view. Consciousness gains a distance from its objects, and discovers its own control over them. Individual
artists create their own versions of the reigning myths to
which they sign their individual names. These versions are
no longer lived, but gazed upon in the theater. The myth is
reduced to the level of literature. It is now no longer transcendent. It is an artifact, the work of man.

This involves a basic change in the structure of consciousness, exemplified in the thought and life of Socrates, where Western history has clearly begun. The mythical man asks no questions. Socrates questions himself and others and indeed all things, bringing them all before the eye of the mind where they can be objectively studied as what they really and essentially are for *any* mind. He examines himself in this way, and says that the unexamined life is not worth living. He is aware of something divine transcending him, but he finds this within himself, in the demonic voice that warns him against certain acts, and in the reason which speaks through this voice. Like the man of myth, he senses a vast order around him, a divine law which allots to all things their place, but he has faith that something of this divine law may be learned, so that virtue may be taught. But he knows nothing of this vast objective order, and is in fact ignorant of the real nature of all things.

The mythical unity has dissolved, and each region of human care, from the humbler arts like horsemanship and shoemaking through medicine, rhetoric, and religion, to the supreme art of wisdom, is now free to develop itself according to its own intrinsic norms, and is the subject of a special mode of dialogue. Politics is no exception. It, too, is a distinct kind of art, quite separate from religion. Socrates' *daimon* warns him against a life of politics as foreign to the wisdom he seeks, and he obeys. But in the end, he is accused of a serious political crime against the Athenian tradition, is condemned, and yields to its authority. He is finally put to death by political judges, an act, as we shall see, that is rich with symbolism for the future. He talks to individuals on the streets and in the market place, but seems more interested in the universal thoughts which his maieutic art brings forth from them. He advises men to tend their souls in order to find the timeless truths that lie within them.

He is certainly an individual, and his life is of critical

importance in our history. But it is the abstractions of justice and truth in which he is primarily interested. History is emerging almost inadvertently and by accident. It is dealt with in mythical tales, but no discourse is devoted exclusively to it. As the Laws say in the *Crito:* "Think not of life and children first . . . but of justice first that you may be justified before the princes of the world below." [14] History emerges only as the background for a rational thought which transcends and envelops it. At best one can say that the relation between the two is left unclear. This also is of prophetic significance for the course of Western history.

There are other suggestive factors in the life of Socrates, but we have no time here to develop them. These are the ones that have taken root. So we must be content with them. Let us now examine them briefly one by one, noting how they were expressed in the thought of Plato and Aristotle, and then how they were developed in the course of our Western history.

From the time of Socrates and Plato, who advised the philosopher to get out of the Cave, little disciplined attention has been paid to human existence as it is lived in the *Lebenswelt.* Such immediate knowledge is dismissed as subjective and unreliable, and an almost exclusive emphasis is placed on what the Greeks called *nous* or reason. This faculty is always understood in terms of metaphors taken from sight which cannot see the eye or anything in close contact, but which gazes at things from a distance, and thus gains a sweeping view of the surfaces. Reason also gazes at objects lying before the mind from a detached point of view. In this way, it apprehends certain traits, or properties, which can be seen by *any* mind, but misses what is unique and concrete. As Aristotle said, there is no science of the individual.

These universal natures form a great cosmic order em-

[14] *Crito* 54.

bracing inorganic things at the bottom; plants, animals, and men in the middle; and at the top a supreme law-giver with angelic ministers. This conception favored the establishment of great world empires like those of Alexander and Rome, which attempted to bring all men universally under their sway in an all-embracing, hierarchical order with slaves at the bottom, ordinary citizens in between, and a supreme emperor at the top with underlings and ministers. The Stoics actually thought of the objective universe as a great city or cosmopolis of which all men are really citizens. The individual was free to suppress his subjective feelings and desires, and to fit them into the cosmic order, but not to create or to exist in a world of his own. Such action is against objective nature, and therefore unjustified.

Even the human state is regarded as natural, though possibly aberrant in certain respects. Nevertheless it must be accepted, like the sun and the stars, as part of the natural order, and can rightly demand obedience and legal conduct from every citizen. To act in this regular way, according to the law of nature, is precisely to be free. This rationalistic tendency to subordinate freedom to order, and the individual to the state, conceived as closer to God and divinely grounded, is discernible throughout the whole course of our history. It has been interpreted as a vestige of primitive myth, but this on the whole is unlikely, for it has constantly attended rationalistic thought from the time of Plato and Aristotle to that of Hegel and Marx. The state is larger, more universal, more stable, and finally far more objective than the individual. These intellectualistic norms are sufficient to account for this noteworthy fact.

Christianity, as we shall see, brought a world of a different kind. It was deeply concerned with the human "heart," with the individual and his history. These ideas were developed to some degree in a Platonic context by St. Augustine and the Augustinian tradition. But in the thirteenth century they were submerged in the great Thomistic synthesis which absorbed the individual and his life-world into a fixed, objective hierarchy of natures or essences. When this synthesis broke down it was replaced by two distinct versions of objective thought.

In the first the neglected factor of subjectivity was focused once more in the Cartesian *cogito,* and developed into the different systems of modern idealism. But it is not a limited individual power that works creatively within the human subject to form a historic human world. It is a universal consciousness *(Bewusstsein überhaupt),* the divine reason of classical thought, an absolute spirit, as Hegel called it, which now works creatively in the mind of man. From this point of view, as for Greek thought, the existing individual is only an object caught up in the universal dialectic of world history where the absolute and eternal is realized in and through time and change. Human reason is more closely identified with the divine, and is active rather than passive.

These doctrines are new. But little attention is paid to the individual and his life-world as they are lived from within. The objective takes precedence over the subjective, the permanent over the ephemeral, the universal over the individual. These features of traditional intellectualism are still found in the thought of Hegel and Marx.

The second version is the great proliferation of objective science which has attended the development of technology since the Renaissance. It possesses certain distinctive features which lead us to oppose it to traditional rationalism. Nevertheless it was historically derived from this source. It has abandoned the notion of transcendence and the divine claims of its ancestor, but it exemplifies the same structure of consciousness. Science in the strict sense abstracts from what is subjective and internal, being concerned only with objects that can be brought before the mind and observed from a detached point of view. It ignores what is unique and individual, seeking only for that which is universally true for all observers. Finally it is not interested in the transitory as such but only in constant uniformities, or laws, through which the flux of objective events can be mastered and controlled.

As we have seen, these traits, objectivity, universality, the search for constancy and control through calculation are characteristic of all rationalistic thought. It is this structure of consciousness that has dominated our Western history since the passing of the world of myth.

This world is directed toward a creative mystery that utterly transcends all human thought and power with an ultimate concern. The rationalistic consciousness shies away from this mythical attitude, always trying to separate itself from such engagement, and to reduce it in some way. Thus science places it within an objective frame, and regards it from the outside as a pattern of psychological or social behavior. But this leads to misunderstanding, for as it is lived from the inside it is itself the ultimate frame. In rationalist philosophy we find a different strategy of assimilation and absorption. Thus for both Plato and Aristotle, reason itself was something divine, and philosophy merges with religion. This trend is apparent even in the thought of Aquinas, for whom reason is the divine image of God in man, metaphysics a divine science, and the final end of man (beatitude) a special form of rational insight. In Hegel, this process of absorption is carried through without reservation to its ultimate conclusion. Reason is the divine spirit in man. Philosophy not only absorbs religion into itself as an immediate manifestation but passes beyond it to the absolute idea where its vague and shifting images are eternally clarified and systematized.

Christianity brought with it, as we shall see, an entirely different approach with many mythical elements. So it was finally met by a sharp distinction between reason and faith that has dominated Western theology down to the present day (cf. Chapter III). But this separation has been constantly diluted by intellectualistic encroachments clearly anticipated in the Anselmian formula, faith seeking understanding (*fides quaerens intellectum*) according to which the mythical vagueness and confusion of faith is to be gradually replaced by the clarity and coherence of the intellect. Faith has its own revealing power and its own coherence. But in the history of religious thought, as it is now called, we can see how its concrete and historical elements have been gradually epitomized and generalized by intellectual analysis. Thus the God of Abraham, Isaac, and Jacob becomes the God of the theologians and philosophers. This process has been influenced by another rational distinction, the separation of theory from practice, so that ethics is different from metaphysics, and dogmatic from moral theology. But the domestication of the Deity is apparent at both levels.

On the theoretical plane, the concrete affirmations of myth that arise from the *Lebenswelt*, as expressing a total engagement of man, become articles of faith, dubious propositions to be believed on the basis of an external authority. Then these articles are expanded by rational deduction, and woven into a system of doctrine concerning God, who is now viewed as an object before the mind. In this way, myth and history are slowly transformed into dogma, and dogma into doctrine. Revelation has become a theory.

At the moral level, God ceases to be a source of generosity and creative power. Instead of them, He is envisaged as a cosmic emperor, a *pantokrator*, ruling the whole human world by an elaborate system of abstract laws and principles. These principles make moral calculation possible, and on this reliable basis, both self and social realization may be achieved. Pure Grace sinks into the background, giving way to a system of virtues and vices and merits for human achievement, with God as a watchful and righteous judge.

In this way, the sacred has been organized, arranged, and brought within the range of rational analysis and calculation.

3. The Failure of the Gnostic Enterprise

With the conquest of myth and the coming of rational reflection, human freedom and history are brought into being. Christianity is essentially involved in them and opens them up. But to the gnostic consciousness which seeks for order and necessity in its objects, they are a threat and an impediment. Freedom, as Kant recognized decisively, is no object, and cannot be understood from an objective point of view. Hence rationalistic thinkers, like Spinoza, making no concession to the evidence of choice, simply exclude it from their deterministic systems. Others, with more respect for world facts, place it as a mysterious and elusive factor within a fixed, cosmic frame where its random acts can at least be held in leash.

Thus for Aristotle and Aquinas, the cosmic order is already established. Man has no freedom to form the world in which he exists. He is free only to follow the guidance of reason in adjusting himself to things as they already are and must be. He does possess a freedom of choice. But this choice cannot affect the structure of the world, and moves within very narrow limits. The ultimate end of man is fixed by nature and divine decree. His choice is restricted to the contingent means which may lead to this end. In Hegelian thought, individual freedom is a subordinate moment in the dialectic of world history which moves according to objective laws of its own. This placing of freedom *within* the structure of a cosmic framework is typical of gnostic thought in the West.

History also is a continuous threat because of its erratic and unpredictable contingency. That the contours of a woman's face should launch a thousand ships and change the course of history is a scandal to the gnostic mind. Hence for a long time after Plato, aside from the great religious adventure of Augustine, history was generally ignored, and not recognized as an academic discipline until the modern period. But in dealing with this aberrant phenomenon, reason, recognizing its danger, often follows an interesting and indirect technique. To plunge into history in its entirety without a key is obviously to be lost. So it is broken down into separate structures each of which can be defined and whose history can then be clearly traced. Thus we can study the history of the sandworm or the horse, the typewriter or the sewing machine, the history of an idea, or even a political structure like democracy. The implication of this procedure is that history can be placed within a frame of stable essences each of which can then be exactly analyzed and defined.

Within such a frame, the flux of passage becomes more intelligible in terms of retrogression and advance toward a permanent goal. But what if the world itself is historical? If so, history cannot be included within any frame. Rather all essential frames of every order are included within an ultimate, *moving* horizon. This idea is unacceptable to the gnostic mind. Hence since the time of Hegel, it has devoted itself persistently to a significant enterprise known as the philosophy of history. There is nothing really new in this modern enterprise. Many great thinkers of the past have formulated exhaustive systems claiming to embody timeless truths and definitive answers to basic questions, impervious to the tooth of time. But as we all know, these claims have proved to be groundless. Human history has gone on to transcend and to encompass them. The so-called philosophy of history is merely the last phase of this struggle to overcome history.

It may indeed possess a wider grasp of historic fact and a deeper sense of the ubiquity of history. These claims may keep it alive for a long time to come. It may be viewed as a last expression of the Western religion of reason. Indeed for many people today this hope for a gnostic discovery of the meaning of history expresses their ultimate concern. But this hope is doomed. Our human reason is a contingent occurrence that happens in time. It cannot climb out of history to attain a timeless truth. As our history now shows all too clearly, it is human—all too human. The vast tangle and sequence of world events and histories will never be embraced within a system of timeless concepts. Rather all such systems will themselves be embraced and transcended.

This is clearly suggested by the history of reason itself in the West. After the breakdown of mythical life and its unity of transcendence, the different modes of human care were free to develop themselves without any check, each in its own way, in its own particular region. Art, science, education, religion, and technology separated themselves from the original unity which had once held them together, and also from one another. It was reason which had ended the reign of myth, and reason, of course, was ideally one and universal. So rational philosophy assigned to itself the task of recovering in its own way the lost unity of myth. This task must be achieved by man the rational animal, either by the individual man alone, or by social man in the state.

From a gnostic point of view the results have not been reassuring.

The overarching unity of reason has not been achieved by the individual. With the passing of the ages of myth, quarrels soon broke out among individual thinkers concerning what should succeed it. And these quarrels have persisted with a few brief interruptions throughout the whole of our Western history. One who looks carefully at this history of philosophy can see in it breadths, depths, soaring visions, and lasting insights. But one cannot see oneness and universality. These are conspicuously absent. If we seriously ask ourselves what spirit this history expresses, it would seem to be rather the spirit of personal freedom than the unified spirit of reason. One speaks confidently of a perennial philosophy, but only by forgetting or discounting one half or one third of this history. We find the reasons of Plato, Aristotle, Democritus, Panaetius, Scotus, Spinoza, and Kant. We do not find universal reason itself, the divine reason in man which will encompass all things, including God, and bring them into a comprehensive and timeless unity. This task has not yet been achieved by any individual, and if we are to judge by past achievement, the prospects are not bright.

But perhaps we are expecting too much from the limited individual. To see these limits is only rational. Let us then consider the vast co-operative enterprise of science on which many now stake their hopes. By its objective method of hypothesis, deduction, and experiment it covers every region of our experience, and arrives at universal results that can be verified by any qualified observer. Certain philosophers dream of a unity of science, but as yet this unity is not seen, only an ever-proliferating diversity of disciplines, no one of which can now be perfectly mastered in a single human life. So even here the hopes for unity are not bright. But even if these hopes were realized in a unity of science finally stable and complete, this would not satisfy the comprehensive demands of reason. In such a synthesis certain very important factors would be omitted—personal existence as it is lived from within, for example. Strict science is not interested in the "subjective." It could not tell us the meaning of the world in which we live, on which all other meanings depend, though this has some importance. There is no science of the world. Finally it could not penetrate to the meaning of history, for there is no science of history. Magnificent as its achievements are, science by itself cannot give us what we need, or even satisfy the needs of reason. So we must look further.

Let us then turn to social man. He also bears a kind of reason which we find in public opinion, tradition, language, and indeed in the life of every civilization. Hegel had a very high opinion of this social reason, which he called *objectiver Geist*, and ranked higher than the subjective thought of the rebellious individual. He held that it is quite distinct from individual existence, and develops in its own way according to rational laws of its own. Since the state is bigger, more objective, more stable, and more universal than the fragile individual, many thinkers have shared his view that here a higher kind of reason is to be found. At this point we should remember Socrates, who started this whole development, though he also glimpsed others not ever tried.

He warned us against politics,[15] and we must not forget that it was the state which put Socrates to death.

If reason in the individual is contaminated by his accidental interests, in the state it suffers from impurities that are even more degrading. Here we find no single universal reason but many *raisons d'état* fused with the special interests of a given society for its own realization and expansion. There is more power here, but not more reason undefiled. At the present time this power has grown to such a degree that, like Socrates, we all face the threat of extinction at the hands of these social monsters whose calculating *raisons d'état* lead them on to a seemingly unlimited self-expansion. Social reason is at least as impure and variable as individual reason. We shall soon see that it is more so. But now we must conclude by returning to the quest of Socrates, which has not ended.

We have seen how he grew up in a time that had freed itself from the reign of myth. He assisted in this process of liberation, and inaugurated a great inquiry, which we have

[15] Plato *Apology* 31C ff.

named the gnostic enterprise, to replace the ambiguities and contradictions of mythical thought by the clarity and coherence of objective reason. This enterprise was directed toward a timeless truth ordered together in a marvelous unity. By the divine reason present in man, this truth might illumine the natures of all things, including the nature of the divine itself. On the wings of such knowledge, we might soar to a firm position beyond the world of man. From here it might be placed within a stable frame, and the meaning of history comprehended. Who knows what Socrates saw in the night when he stood in a trance on the eve of the battle of Delium? In the light of such comprehension elicited from the souls of men, sound guidance might be given to their free action both as individuals and as cities.

Perhaps this was the dream of Socrates. At least it was so interpreted, and has been so interpreted for two thousand years. Now at last we can see that this great quest has failed to achieve the ultimate aims of its enthusiastic adherents. And we can imagine how Socrates, if he were here with us, after delving into the great works of our philosophy, after questioning our well-known thinkers, and after learning of our predicament, might once again say, as he said once before: "The truth is, O men of the modern world, that God alone is wise . . . and the wisdom of men is worth little or nothing." [16] The message of Socrates is ambiguous, as even our history shows. He inaugurated the great gnostic quest of which we have been speaking. No doubt it was worth while within certain limits we are learning to understand, but our hopes for its ultimate triumph have somewhat dimmed. Certainly we cannot return to the age of myth.

But there is another possibility which he may also have glimpsed, as some of his interpreters believe. This possibility has never been really tried, and to this we shall turn in our next chapter.

[16] *Ibid.*, 23A.

Chapter Two

CHRISTIANITY, MYTH, AND RATIONALISM

In the last chapter we considered the critical passage which lies at the root of our Western history from mythical life to rational thought and existence. We have noted the deep sense of transcendence and the global grasp of the life-world which belong to the former, but also its lack of personality, freedom, and historicity which called for a revolutionary change. With the passing of the age of myth, personal freedom and history were brought into being. But we have also seen how the gnostic enterprise, as we have called it, which was to have guided this rational life, has failed to shed sufficient light. It has failed to illumine the depths of subjectivity. Instead of bringing us closer, it has removed us farther from transcendence. It has been unable to comprehend the freedom and historicity that it has itself unleashed. In all these areas rational men have had to resort to fragmentary myths.

This is enough to show a failure to substantiate its basic claims.

Far from bringing about the last decline of myth, as the positivists of the nineteenth century supposed, they were actually inaugurating a period of unprecedented mythical proliferation. In the twentieth century we have been confronted with religious myths, historical myths, and political myths of vast persuasive power. This is sufficient to reveal a fundamental failure. But more needs to be said. Fragmentary myths are still very much alive in the critical fields where ultimate judgments of value must be made. But the integral myth that unified the life of primitive man has been definitively destroyed, and left to itself, each component factor being free to develop in its own way apart from the rest. Thus the unifying factor of transcendence, no longer fused with the rest of life, has become the special concern of what is called *religion* and has undergone a special institutional history of its own, deeply affected by the prevailing attitudes of rationalistic thought.

Hence the penetrating critique of reason inaugurated by Kant at the end of the Enlightenment has often been taken to be at the same time a destructive critique of religion, and one has wondered whether religion could survive the decline of rationalism in the West. The very existence of prehistoric myth is enough to suggest an affirmative answer to this question. Nevertheless, in view of the close connection between Western religion and rational theology in our history such questions continue to be raised. Is religion essentially dependent on rational argument and calculation? Can it be more broadly defined? If so, what is this broader definition? To these questions we shall now turn in the following section. After this, we shall consider a special form of religion, Christian faith, and the ways in which it differs from myth as well as from rationalism.

1. *What Is Religion?*

In intellectual circles the word "God" suggests the absolute of objective philosophy whose being can be demonstrated by rational argument. An atheist is one who rejects the conclusion of such arguments. In this sense, of course, there are many atheists, and many cogent arguments can indeed be offered on their side. A "reason" which could work out such a demonstration would be leading us to the divine, and would itself have to partake of the divine. One finds in fact that many rationalists have identified reason with God in this way. Thus Aristotle speaks of *nous* as a divine element in man,[1] and Aquinas refers to the metaphysics which develops such arguments as "a divine science." [2] But can this claim be justified?

Our human "reason" seems to be inextricably bound up with the rest of us, and equally subject to the limits of our humanity. How can such a weak and fragile faculty escape from this finitude to identify us with something altogether transcendent? Furthermore, demonstration is a calculation which, in so far as it succeeds, gives us a certain control over its object. At least it gives us access which is a kind of control. But is this really compatible with the transcendence of a mystery?

The rational philosopher wishes to base his theories on constraining evidence before the mind, and to eliminate the uncertainty of faith. But this enterprise is never finished, and itself rests on a hope. The arguments of natural theology depend on certain concepts, like that of being, whose meaning is not clear, and on certain premises, like that of sufficient reason, which are not evident. Far from giving faith a firm foundation on indubitable, rational evidence, these arguments for the existence of God belong to an uncertain and unfinished enterprise which itself rests on a kind of faith.

Other questions may be raised concerning the object of such demonstrations. Is God an object, or a thing, possessing certain traits that can be brought before the mind, and certain causal connections with other things? If so, He can

---

[1] *Nichomachean Ethics* x. 1177ᵇ 27.
[2] Cf. Anderson, *Metaphysics of St. Thomas Aquinas* (Chicago: Regnery, 1953), chap. x, where most of the relevant texts are assembled.

be demonstrated, as anthropologists can demonstrate that men of intelligence were existing at a certain time because of the presence of certain artifacts in a given stratum of rock. We say that men are connected with artifacts by an objective, causal law, as the pressure of a gas is causally connected with its volume. Hence from the existence of artifacts, we can infer the objective existence of men like ourselves.

But this is an error.

Men like ourselves exist in the world subjectively from the inside. This existence cannot be observed from the outside as a fact, but only directly as lived from within, or by concrete encounter and sympathy. It is true that artifacts are found in a human world. But they are not "caused"; they are made for a purpose that fits a certain way of life. It is true that by historical sympathy and imagination I may reconstruct a primitive world from its artifacts. But this is not a "causal" inference from one thing (utensil) to another thing (man). It is the historical interpretation of a past stage of the world in which I now exist, which rests on my understanding of this present world and is continuous with it. Furthermore this understanding is not objective, for my world is not an object. But I have a lived awareness of it as the horizon of my existence.

If man is not a thing which can be adequately understood objectively in the third person and demonstrated by logic, it is hard to believe that God is something of this kind. If so, He can no more be proved by a "causal" type of argument than the concrete existence of a human person can be "proved" in this way. Such existence can be revealed only by direct confrontation, encounter, and historic witness which require sympathetic understanding and interpretation. But if God has been encountered and witnessed in human history, this witness can no longer be interpreted in terms of the world that we know, for He transcends this human world.

He is not an object, but a mystery that envelops us subjectively as well as objectively. Hence such interpretation
must lie beyond the limits of human science and philosophy.

If this is true, it is certainly false to identify atheism with
those who reject logical arguments for the existence of God.
As a matter of fact, such rejections often arise from religious
apprehensions of the holy that are closer to this mysterious
phenomenon than any arguments. The fact that philosophers, engaged in the enterprise of embracing the whole of
being in a rational system, have been led to recognize transcendence as a rational necessity is certainly significant. God
is the faith of reason realized, an infinite understanding in
which all epistemological problems are resolved. This ideal
underlies the whole intellectual enterprise. It expresses what
the philosopher would be like if he ever achieved his final
aim.

But the most significant phase of this endeavor is its
inevitable failure.

The attempt to understand God in terms of concepts
breaks down because God is not a conceptual object. The
attempt to infer his existence by causal arguments breaks
down because He is not a thing. Every act of man is finite,
and when really pressed, it reaches a limit beyond which it
cannot pass. The God of the philosophers, as Pascal called
this strange phenomenon, shows the way in which Western
thinkers have sensed this limit to their discursive methods.
It is the expression of philosophic faith. These divinities of
Aquinas, Descartes, Leibnitz and Kant are not like those
of the East. Every rational theology, whether Eastern or
Western, refers to a God already "known" in another way.
In spite of their differences, it is amazing how much our
philosophical deities actually resemble the God of Christian
revelation. The rational need has passed its limit still unsatisfied, and is feeling and struggling for a transcendent
answer. This "answer" is the expression of a searching philo-

sophic faith. Here lies its true significance. But in so far as it tries to defend this answer as a clear demonstration of factual existence and a thorough calculation of fixed properties, it only reveals its limits once more in an inadvertent way. This rational projection is not the living God. It is rather the academic reflection of a philosophic need that still remains unanswered. To reject this pale construction is not atheism. It is rather the expression of a still living religious faith.

Recent theological criticism has shown that the traditional interpretation of religious faith as the acceptance of propositions, or articles, about an objective Deity altogether fails to do justice to Christian faith, or to the way of life involved in any world religion.[3] This is amply confirmed by recent anthropological and phenomenological studies.[4] To take account of this evidence it is now essential to widen our traditional conception of religion both objectively and subjectively. The idea of God as an object which must be indirectly inferred from empirical facts is a late and highly specialized conception. If we are to avoid provincialism, and even sectarianism, we must recognize rather that the sacred, or the holy, which lies at the root of all religion, far from being an interpretation added to, or an inference based on experience is rather something directly encountered in our lived experience of the *Lebenswelt*. It is a power, wholly other than man and veiled in mystery, which inspires wonder and awe. This is the "object" of religious adoration.

Theoretical contemplation may be a peripheral aspect of this response, or a highly specialized manifestation of it. What is common to all religion, however, is an attitude of total devotion or concern. In more advanced forms of wor-

[3] Cf. R. Mehl, *La Condition du philosophe Chrétien* (Paris: Delachaux and Niestlé, 1947), pp. 27–28.
[4] Cf. Eliade, *op. cit.;* and Van der Leeuw, *Phänomenologie der Religion,* especially pp. 506–508.

ship, the religious "object" is an enveloping mystery which transcends the objective as well as the subjective aspects of the individual's world. It is that which has led all reflective persons, and indeed all cultures, to distinguish between *their* worlds and *the* common world which transcends and reduces them all to special perspectives. These living world religions call the subject to an attitude of ultimate devotion to which everything else is subordinated.

To do justice to this array of evidence now gathered from many sources, we must, therefore, think of religion in a much broader way as the ultimate devotion to a transcendent mystery directly encountered in the concrete world of existence. Christianity is in this sense a religion, of which our rationalist philosophy, with its many subvarieties, is a very special and perhaps highly diluted expression. But there are many other forms which we cannot ignore. If this broader conception is accepted, what we now call *atheism* turns out to be itself a derived religious phenomenon, not at all the absence of religion, but rather, as we have suggested, the movement away from a rationalist mode of worship, which is itself essentially religious. This insight, now clearly emerging from recent phenomenology, is often misunderstood. Hence it is worthy of some brief attention.

Living faith is always mixed with incredulity, and psychoanalysis has taught us to see that hate is the counterpart of love. An impassioned denial rests on an affirmation that is still alive. One who is wholly indifferent to God, if there is such a one, does not blaspheme. Alfred de Musset expressed this very well in the story he tells of the "atheist" who, "drawing out his watch, gave God a quarter of an hour to destroy him. He thus procured for himself fifteen minutes of dreadful anger and joy. It was a paroxysm of despair, a nameless appeal to all the celestial powers. Here is a poor and miserable creature writhing under the foot which is to tread him down. Here is a cry of anguish. And who knows?

In the eyes of Him who sees all, perhaps this is a prayer." [5]

In our religious history we find many critics of the failures of the established Church, its disregard for the corruption of its members, its indifference to social justice, etc. Such attacks, however, arise from a serious concern for purity and justice. Hence they are not properly interpreted as atheistic. Though they may try to negate any element of transcendence and mystery, their hope for a righteous future, unlike anything as yet experienced, is grounded on something dimly discerned that is neither exactly explained nor clearly expressed. What is this if not a mystery? Similar hopes may be discerned as crucial elements in great "antireligious" movements of our time, such as scientism and Marxism, though usually concealed by deceptive arguments and polemics.

Thus the positivist may argue that religious experience is an abnormal psychological phenomenon conditioned by neurological disease. But as James pointed out long ago, in his Gifford lectures of 1902,[6] this violates the established rules of scientific and empirical procedure. "In the natural sciences and industrial arts it never occurs to anyone to try to refute opinions by showing up their author's neurotic constitution." If every scientist and psychologist had to establish his own perfect freedom from psychosomatic disturbance before his theories could be examined, the advance of these disciplines would be slow indeed. Many of the most important discoveries might be soon discredited in this way. If such an indirect procedure is unacceptable in science, it should not be applied to religion. In all religions, if we are to proceed empirically, a theory must be tested directly in terms of its immediate luminousness in the light of the evidence, its relation to what is already known, and the relevance of its ultimate presuppositions. What lies back of the positivistic urge to fit every

[5] *La Confession d'un enfant du siecle,* quoted in G. Gusdorf, *Traité de métaphysique* (Paris: Colin, 1956), p. 416.
[6] *Varieties of Religious Experience* (New York: Modern Library, 1953), p. 19.

phenomenon into the objective framework of science? Is this not a millennarian hope which goes far beyond anything as yet achieved? Can the ground of this hope be clearly explained and justified? Is it anything more than one possible mode of response to an ultimate mystery?

The same questions can be raised concerning the ultimate faith of Marxism, and the answer is even clearer. Here there is a marked parallelism with corresponding structures of Judaeo-Christian faith which strikes the eye at once—the millennarian hope for a classless society beyond all known experience, and the sacrificial role of the messianic proletariat. No doubt this form of faith has its own distinctive features and its own peculiar difficulties. But how can we fail to see that it is the expression of an ultimate concern in the face of mystery, and therefore a phenomenon essentially religious in character?

This is even true of the sense of the Divine absence which is a noteworthy manifestation of the broken thought of our own time. God was once closer to us, but from our over-populated world of facts, statistics, and machines, He has somehow withdrawn. To many of our contemporaries, the traditional liturgies are a hollow ceremonial whose purely human significance is all too evident. No tools to which we now have access are capable of bringing us nearer to the Divine. It seemed that God once spoke to us. Now He is silent. But in such expressions there is a note of nostalgia. God is dead *to us*. From our world He has retired. These expressions are far from a consistent atheism.

According to other thinkers, this vacant place is to be filled by man. This conception can be traced back to certain followers of Hegel in the nineteenth century, like Feuerbach and Max Stirner whose exasperated reflections on the solitary individual, though unjustly neglected, anticipated many radical phases of the humanism of our time.[7]

[7] M. Stirner (pseud. J. K. Schmidt), *The Ego and his Own*, trans. Byington (New York: Boni and Liveright, 1918).

God is dead. In fact we have killed Him, for He stood in the way of our own self-transcendence, and reduced us to a state of servility. This Nietzschean theme is now resumed by Sartre, who wishes to replace theology by a new anthropology "so that man may recover that creative liberty which Descartes attributed to God, and so that one may at last surmise that final truth which lies at the root of humanism: man is the one whose appearance brings a world into being." [8] On this view, there is certainly a factor of ultimate concern, for man cares for his own self-creation. But how about the factor of mystery? This envelopes us and lies beyond us, transcending all our categories. It both attracts us and repels us, neither opposing our poor efforts nor assisting them. It is neither meaningless nor meaningful. Nevertheless it can be understood, at least to some degree, as what it is—a mystery. As such, it seems to be penetrable, but not penetrated. It does not merely ward us off. It beckons as well. This is mystery when it is freely faced and not evaded or denied.

If this happens, it takes on another form, as may be seen in the case of Sartre and other existentialist writers who deny all mystery and try to put man in its place. Mystery still envelops us and the world in which we exist, as a brute factuality in which we are simply thrown. Instead of transcending us, it now appears as a subhuman contingency opposing our efforts in the form of chance, and shattering us in the end. Instead of being beyond what is meaningful for us, it is now entirely opaque and meaningless, resisting our understanding completely and from the very start. This is the category of *the absurd,* mystery as it appears to the Sartrian man becoming God. From this point of view it can be reduced and distorted. But it cannot be removed.

In the light of these considerations, we may be able to see that irreligion and atheism are far rarer than is com-

[8] *Situations* (Paris: Gallimard, 1947–49), I, 334.

monly supposed. Have we done justice to agnosticism? it may be asked. It is true that sheer indifference approaches this ideal limit more closely than any form of blasphemy, or active enmity toward faith. But serious questions may be raised as to whether this limit can ever be really attained. Herbert Spencer, the philosopher of agnosticism, finally reached the concept of the unknowable, as he called it, which he found he could not escape. This concept turns out to have much in common with what we have called mystery. The agnostic would seem to be one who is really concerned to guard this mystery against false solutions and confusions, a religious purist of a certain kind. A man who, like W. K. Clifford, refuses to accept any easy answer and insists on withholding judgment until decisive evidence can be found, is devoting himself to an ultimate ideal of verified knowledge which can be accepted on faith but not fully justified, since it transcends any evidence we have attained. The indifferentist who sees the weakness of all faith and struggles against any final commitment, is committing himself finally to a mysterious ideal of freedom that no man has ever seen.

It is true that religion is absent from many perspectives which we can take. It is certainly absent from the objective universe of science, except in a barren and truncated form. But it seems to be present in the actual life-world of concrete existence, and indeed as a necessary dimension of this concrete world. Here we are confronted with an ultimate mystery which may or may not be focused in distinct phenomena or events, and this ultimate mystery calls for an ultimate concern of some kind.

Indeed there is no known culture where such concern is not found, and as we have seen, only very few, if any, individuals of advanced cultures have succeeded in escaping it. Cogent evidence for this is found in the distinction between the world of a people or a culture and *the* world as such, which is due to a recognition of transcendence and is recognized everywhere.

In the broad sense we have given it, as concern for an ultimate mystery, religion cannot be essentially identified with rational theology. It is rather a dimension of human existence. Religious concern may take an indefinite number of alternative forms, including that of myth. No one can be taken without danger and risk. But each culture and each individual face such a choice. Some one must be taken, and on the way in which this choice is exercised, the structure of a human world will then depend. Christianity is one such choice now open to us. If our account so far has been correct, as a type of religious response, it must be generally distinguished from any rational scheme of concepts with which it may from time to time become associated. But this leaves the question of myth still open.

How is Christian faith related to myth?

We shall consider this question in the following section (2). After this, in the light of our discussion, we shall offer an interpretation of Christian faith which we believe is relevant to our time (3). Finally (4) we shall examine certain special ways in which it differs from gnostic thought.

2. Christianity and Myth

The gnostic enterprise has failed. So let us now turn to a third possibility with which we are familiar in many versions both mythological and rational, but with whose pure and unadulterated forms we are only beginning to become acquainted. We place it under a special, rational category, religion, and thus divide it from other "fields" like education, philosophy, hygiene, and technology. This in itself is a misunderstanding which has prevented wider implications from being fully understood or even explored. It was not meant to be religion in our present sense, but, like primitive myth, a total way of life and thought. Nevertheless it cannot be identified with either the integral myth of primitive society or with the fragmentary myths of Western history. Let us now try to clarify these important distinctions.

The things that we deal with in ordinary experience are not things as they are in themselves apart from us. They are rather these things in relation to us, as they are revealed by our thought and feeling. The personal self is the center of this world-horizon which one carries with him wherever he goes. But this self does not exist apart from the world. It exists only in so far as it reveals itself as the center of this world which includes many beings quite independent of it. This experience as a whole may be compared to a dialogue between two independent persons who exist for each other only in terms of an interfused pattern of question and response.

The world of Christianity must be understood in the same way as a complex of interactions and meanings arising between two independent beings, a dialogue between God and man. But of this world, transcendence is the center. Man and his *Lebenswelt* play only a subordinate role. The word *God* refers to God as He reveals Himself in relation to man, here understood in relation to God or as responding to Him. This is a bipolar structure, neither pole having meaning without the other. Thus the divine act toward man is referred to as *revelation,* and the human response as *faith.* But each can be understood only in relation to the other, as a question calls for the answer, and an answer responds to the question. In the same way, revelation calls for faith, and faith responds to revelation, neither being meaningful alone.

Faith is not a doctrine about God, including certain moral prescriptions which are then to be lived out in the world as it is. It is rather a total response to certain historical events which call for a reorientation of the world toward God, and not any more around man. This call for reorientation has often been interpreted as a call to another world, leaving this world behind and intact. But this is a misunderstanding. The human life-world is neither denied nor left behind. Revelation is made through historic events in this world, and leaves it fully intact. What is required is not a departure but a recentering of the world of man. It is true that a recentered world is very different. But the man of faith still exists in the *Lebenswelt* with the rest of us, facing the same catastrophes and suffering the same pains. He is making no effort to escape. He is trying rather to reorient himself, and lives in a constant tension between two centers, himself and God.

The Christian religion certainly tells of an encounter between God and men. In this respect it resembles the myths of primitive societies and even the fragmentary myths of history and politics which continue to appear in our Western history, like the Nazi myth of blood and soil and the master race. These, too, involve a fictive account of human events with at least a tacit reference to transcendence. But there are certain characteristics which distinguish the Christian Bible from myths of both kinds.

The fragmentary myths that have occurred in our history, and are still occurring, do not require a radical reorientation of the whole human world to a transcendent center. Like the Nazi myth, the humanist-religious myth of Auguste Comte, and mythical interpretations of national origins and survivals, they rather claim to give transcendent support to certain human movements and aspirations which may have world-wide ramifications, but which are nevertheless contained within the human world horizon which is presupposed by the movement in question. Thus the Nazi or Marxist aim of world mastery or world reform must remain within the given world, or become quite meaningless. Christianity, however, calls for a complete reorientation of the world around a transworldly center. This distinguishes it from those fragmentary myths, as we have called them, with which we are familiar in Western history.

This does not serve to distinguish it, however, from those forms of mythical life which we examined in the last chapter, and which orient the whole of human existence toward something transcendent. But here we may notice several differences.

a. The global myth of primitive culture does not appear in a world already ordered around man as the center by reason and technology. It does not exist in dialectical tension with such a world. The primitive myth constitutes the only world there is for the primitive society.

b. This myth is understood impersonally and collectively by the society. Christianity, on the other hand, is addressed to free, self-conscious persons.

c. As we have seen, the global myth is beyond time and ahistorical. Christian faith, on the other hand, is essentially involved in human events that occurred in human history, and exists in this history.

d. The myth has no place for rational reflection and breaks down before serious questioning. Authentic faith, however, has prepared itself to meet such questioning, and requires a full development of reason for mastery over the animals and the earth.

e. Finally, and most important of all, as we have seen, the mythical world is frozen and closed to all creative reconstruction. Christian faith, however, in the Bible is compared to a leaven. For it, all things are to become new. Hence it is free and open not only to a deepening self-correction of itself, but to a development and renewal of all human fields and occupations. These differences make it clear that a sharp distinction between Christian faith and myth is thoroughly justified.

These remarks, however, require a certain qualification. The Bible is concerned with human existence in the world of man. As recent phenomenological study has shown,[9] it expresses many insights into the nature of this existence in the ordinary language of mankind from which all technical languages develop, and in terms of which they must be finally understood. Such language is concrete and filled with many references which are only incidental, and peculiar to the atmosphere and life of the time. So far as they can be understood by later generations, they must be translated into another concrete language relative to another time. As this process is repeated, what is essential in this message concerning the life-world is apt to be confused with what is only incidental, and thus distorted and misunderstood.

If by myth we mean, as we now generally do, any concrete statement, or expression, whose accepted meaning is largely fictional and untrue, then certain Biblical statements about man are mythical, as we know, for example, that the Aramaic word for life was translated into Greek as soul (psyche) which conveys to us an erroneous impression concerning human existence.[10] In cases of this sort, linguistic study, together with phenomenology and anthropology, can perform an important service in purifying or demythologizing, in this very general sense, the message of the Gospel.

The Bible and the tradition of the Church also tell us about historical events. But this knowledge of history, always based on memory and personal, human interpretation, is necessarily limited and relative to the special situation of the time. Here again tradition may not only preserve historic truth but accident as well, and may often confuse the two. In this way, mistaken interpretations, or myths, may arise.

[9] Cf. S. Kierkegaard, *Concluding Unscientific Postscript*, trans. Swenson (Princeton University Press, 1944); and M. Heidegger, *Sein und Zeit* (Halle: Niemeyer, 1927).
[10] Cf. R. Bultmann, *Theology of the New Testament*, trans. Grobel (New York: Scribners, 1951–55), I, 203–205.

Disciplined historical research in such cases may render a vital service to faith in correcting mistakes, and in bringing it closer to the events themselves and their original significance.

But the elimination of mythical accretions from the anthropological parts of this message is only a beginning. It must also be understood in the light of such knowledge as we may obtain from a free examination of the evidence available to all. The task of obtaining such knowledge belongs to philosophical anthropology and the sciences of man. Underlying these disciplines, however, there are certain ultimate meanings such as being, truth, consciousness, value, and transcendence which must be clarified so far as possible.

This task belongs to first-philosophy or metaphysics. The evidence here is so rich and ambiguous that while lasting truths may be attained, final solutions are impossible. Hence this philosophic task must be reassumed and renewed by each generation in its own historic situation. It is concerned with the meaning of human existence, and the mystery of transcendence. Hence every Christian theologian, and indeed every Christian, must be vitally concerned with it. Unless it is free to follow the human evidence wherever it may lead with no external constraint, it loses its grip on the truth accessible to it, and becomes a mere handmaid. It can be neither separated from theology nor easily united with it. The two must live and develop rather in a constant tension with each other which may be destructive or fruitful, depending on the insight of those who pursue these disciplines and the situation of their time.

Faith cannot be separated from philosophy. Nevertheless it has its own kind of evidence, and its own distinctive modes of understanding which are not to be confused with those of reason. This understanding exists in the minds and hearts of living men and must, therefore, like philosophy, be regenerated and renewed in each generation. This may result in decay or decline. On the other hand, it may result in growth, which may take two forms, either theological or philosophical. Theology is the critical reflection of faith on itself, which may lead to deeper understanding. This is the first form of growth. Or faith may be led by philosophy to reflect creatively on its relation to new problems and new situations in history. This is the second form of growth. Times of rapid social change are apt to call forth such reflection.

We are living in such a time of technological advance, social upheaval, and conflict which have elicited from man a new understanding of himself. This development is reflected in the new philosophy of existence which has now taken root in all parts of the Western world. This has elicited a response from faith which is now developing in the two ways just noted. Not only is it reflecting on certain new problems brought forth by scientific advance, like *euthanasia* and *genocide;* it is also reflecting on itself. As a result of this, the meaning of its basic symbols is undergoing reinterpretation and transformation. We shall take some account of these changes in an interpretation of Christian symbols which we shall now try briefly to suggest.

3. *A Contemporary Interpretation of the Basic Christian Symbols*

The Christian creed was traditionally referred to as a symbol, and we are now following this usage. But by the term *symbol* we mean a physical object, or expression, in which transcendence becomes transparent to faith. A religious symbol is not the same as a sign. A sign refers to something other than itself which can be approached in other ways. Thus smoke is the sign of a fire which can be known directly apart from smoke. But the symbol refers to a mystery which can be approached in no other way. This symbol may, of course, be interpreted, but only through other finite symbols which are not the mystery. Nevertheless it may reveal itself in them, and even be present in them to faith. The meaning inhabits the symbol but also transcends it.[11] Hence in performing its act the symbol vanishes. When understood in the light of faith, the words of the creed become transparent to transcendence and vanish in mystery. Each generation must then interpret them. But each of these interpretations, while perhaps more relevant to the life and thought of the time, is itself only another symbol.

Let us now try to construct such an interpretation adapted to our own situation in history, and, therefore, able to remove clouds in the glass, and perhaps to clear it for living men today. Naturally we have no time for a treatise on theology. We must be content with a few suggestions concerning some symbols in the creed.

I believe in. . . . This beginning of the creed is very significant. Can we not interpret it as implying that the Christian revelation is addressed primarily, though not exclusively, to the existing person (I), who responds by a free act of belief? This belief is not an intellectual affirmation about something, as I may believe *that* the moon is so many miles away. It is rather a belief *in* the integrity of a person known to me by direct encounter and shared existence, as in time of crises, I have faith in the support of a lifelong friend. Such faith is not based on induction, for the situation may be altogether unprecedented. Like the certainty of my own death, it is based rather on an immediate grasp of existential structure.

God the Father Almighty. . . . The term *God* may be interpreted as that ultimate mystery which is in some way, no matter how confused or perverse this may be, involved in the ultimate concern of every man. This mystery can be

[11] Van der Leeuw, *Phänomenologie der Religion,* pp. 503–512.

felt and apprehended in at least two ways: (1) as a result of reflection on the finitude of man and all empirical existence; and (2) as a surplus of meaning still in reserve after every act of comprehension. But this is a unique insight into a unique situation which cannot be derived from any logical argument from wider principles and premises. The next two terms, *Father* and *Almighty,* indicate a dialectical tension which we accept. *Father* refers to a personal existent who cares for his children and is capable of love and mercy. *Almighty,* on the other hand, refers to a transcendent power, both awesome and fascinating, which is beyond all such limits. This term, we believe, deserves the major emphasis. The ultimate object of faith is a mystery beyond all human categories and analogies.[12] But without privation or degeneration, this transcendence can be revealed to us as a father concerned for his children. As the creative source of all being and value, however, He transcends any such analogy. Here again faith is confronted with a dialectical tension. It is given an image to start it on its way, but is warned against taking this image too literally.

Nevertheless it is significant that these guiding images are taken from those family relations where our whole being —biological, social, and personal—is involved. As we now well know, these relations, not as they are regarded from the outside but as they are lived from the inside, provide us with the basic patterns of thought and feeling that underlie our actual existence. It is only by an immediate grasp of our personal existence as we live it in the family that we may gain some distant sense of the source of our being.

The event of the Incarnation itself is understood by faith in terms of a family relation. Jesus is interpreted as the Son of the Father—*His only Son.* This again is only an analogy which points to a mystery beyond. But traditional attempts to spell out this mystery by the use of rational concepts bor-

[12] Cf. R. Otto, *The Idea of the Holy,* trans. Harvey (rev. ed.; London: Oxford University Press, 1936), now a phenomenological classic.

rowed from Greek philosophy have only led us into a maze of further symbols that are less concrete and direct. In our time, it is probably wise to avoid such rationalizations. The relation of Christ to the Divinity we cannot hope to fathom. This is a relation of peculiar personal intimacy involving a certain priority and yet at the same time a fundamental equality. If we think of a father's love for his only son, we shall be led in the right direction. Such a son belongs to the father's being, and any injury to this son is felt as his own. In giving his son for sacrificial action, he is giving up himself. Nevertheless this son is free, and independent, and able to act on his own.

A genuine family cannot be properly understood in its concrete life by the abstract notion of unity. It is not a single thing, or substance, for it is composed of persons who are separate and free. But neither is it an abstract plurality, for these persons are united by the bond of love, so that each one acts with the others and for the others. As St. Augustine pointed out, we cannot by reflection come closer to the Trinity than by thinking of it on the analogy of persons existing together in a community of love.

That he *suffered under Pontius Pilate, was crucified dead and buried,* refer to human events of history which are open to critical study and research. The idea that such affirmations, dependent on contingent events and thus at the mercy of historical scholarship must be accepted, has often been embarrassing to systematic theologians. Nevertheless this embarrassment must be accepted, even with a kind of joy, for it is this essential dependence on historical events that radically separates Christian faith both from metaphysical doctrine and global myth.

At a time when critical research has questioned much of the biographical material in the Gospels, and when mythical conceptions, like that of the Hellenistic divine man, are still prevalent, it is just as important now to emphasize this human historicity as it was in the early centuries of the Church. It is a human life that was lived, bearing in it all the essential marks and limitations of human existence in history. Even though many of the reported facts may have lost their strict biographic significance, enough remains to reveal a personal existence.[13] The notion of some critics that the message alone remains [14] must be rejected. For the message cannot be separated from the person.

The rising from the dead, like any event of historic significance, is not an objective fact that can be demonstrated. It is rather a fact bearing meaning, to which the disciples and their reported acts bear witness. This meaning merges with mystery. Like them, we are called upon in a similar way not to demonstrate or to comprehend but to believe and to bear witness, in thought and word and deed. Certain critics have attempted to identify the resurrection exclusively with this death to old ways and the constant arising of a new life in history.[15] This wholly immanent solution is incomplete, and should, therefore, be rejected. Nevertheless, as we shall see, it calls attention to an essential aspect of New Testament teaching, and must not be neglected. Indeed this immanent teaching has a peculiar relevance and importance for the broken world of our time.

The eschatological passage *He shall come to judge the quick and the dead . . .* also has both a transcendent and an immanent aspect. It is not only eschatology but realized eschatology as well. No doubt, as traditional interpretations have emphasized, it suggests a last end, a meaning, and a direction in history which are beyond all finite comprehension. But it also suggests an immanent presence of Christ in the world, a calling to decision here and now between death and new life in history. It is not merely that an ultimate, objective end is to be imagined and awaited. If all

[13] Cf. M. Goguel, *Jésus* (Paris: Payot, 1950).

[14] Cf. R. Bultmann, *Jesus and the Word,* trans. Smith & Huntress (New York: Scribners, 1934).

[15] Cf. Bultmann, *Theology of the New Testament,* I, 292–306.

things are to end, the individual also will end, together with all his cares and aspirations. In facing his end, the individual will be led to his final possibilities, and to a radical choice between an old way of life which is really death, and a death of the old which is really life. It is only in the light of our final limits, that final choice and authentic existence become possible.

The Holy Ghost is the spirit of sacrifice which can touch the hearts of all men everywhere, which bloweth where it listeth, and can suddenly arise without warning in the most unexpected places. It is the very gift of love which unites the persons of the Trinity. The Church we shall interpret as the living body of Christ enlivened by His presence which extends itself to all who sacrifice themselves in struggling against established evil, and rise again with Him to a new creative existence in history. Into this social body can be brought all the disparate, fragmentary thoughts and aspirations of men moved by the Spirit. Here, no matter how opposed and contradictory they may be, they may be purified of their pride, and ordered together in an integral (*katholon,* catholic) way toward the mystery which transcends them all.

This Church is a concrete institution which lasts throughout the generations. It not only preaches the prophetic word to the free individual, caught in the meshes of his historic situation, but holds these words in a living tradition through time, and holds these individuals and their acts in a sacramental community of worship and devotion. We think that the time has come when the notion of communion should be broadened to include not only those who are nominally members of the Church, but all those who are touched by the Spirit of justice and sacrifice, even those who are ignorant of Christianity, and those who attack the established Churches for their sins and failures in the life of devotion which they profess.

By *the forgiveness of sins,* we should refer not only to that which is given by God in the sacraments of the Church but to that which can be given through the mediation of men in natural life to those who offend against them. It is only in this way that human beings can be freed from the terrible burdens of the past, and released for creative existence. Unless the lonely child, and the outcast who lives in every man, are received and forgiven, they will fall either into a dead routine or a chaos of distraction which are both the expression of hopeless despair.

The resurrection of the body is a mystery only dimly penetrated by the light of faith. It is very important, however, to take account both of the results of Biblical criticism as well as of the nondualistic thought of our time, and, therefore, to avoid confusing this assertion of Faith with the very different philosophic theory of the natural immortality of the soul.

4. *Christianity and Rationalism*

This, then, is what we mean by Christianity. We do not claim any timeless validity for this interpretation. We believe only that it takes account of the relevant historical facts so far as they are known, as well as of basic truths which may be found in authentic interpretations of the past. We believe that it will be superseded by other interpretations of those coming after us, which will nevertheless take account of the seminal truths contained in it. This is an interpretation of the Christian creed which is now developing in the living thought of those around us in many lands, and which we find to be relevant to our peculiar situation in history. It is, of course, only a brief sketch which we have already clarified to a certain degree by showing how it differs from myth. We shall now try to develop it a little further by showing specific ways in which it differs just as radically from the thought and life of reason.

a. We have seen how the breakdown of mythical life inaugurated an era of openness and freedom which is embodied in the tradition of humanism still living today. Freedom is always *from* something and *to* something else. According to the humanist conception which originated in classical times, the exercise of reason in which true freedom lies is to be achieved by a freedom from irrational passion and bias, and then by an acceptance of cosmic law established by the divine reason in which we share. In following such rational principles, we may find not only peace and security but self-realization as well.[16] With the shattering of the cosmic order in modern times, a new view of freedom appeared on the scene.

Thus Descartes describes a divine, constitutive freedom which is unlimited by any fixed principles, which created not only things but laws and essences, and of which human freedom is the exact image. Kant similarly places human freedom in a new horizon of its own beyond all objective categories and forms of intuition. This new conception, strange to antiquity, of a freedom not caught in the meshes of a world already established but constituting a world of its own, has been clearly grasped and developed only in our own time.[17] As we shall see, it is leading us to a new conception of natural law and social ethics. It has also generated a perverse libertarianism which fails to see its basic world significance.

On this view, a directionless self-realization is to be achieved by an individual in the given world with no constraint of any kind. Freedom may be won simply by rejecting tradition and external authority of any kind, except that of science and technology, which provides the necessary instru-

[16] Cf. Aristotle's discussion of choice in *Nichomachean Ethics* iii. 2–5; and Aquinas' doctrine of *liberium arbitrium, Summa Theologiae* I. qu. 83. For a summary of the humanist conception of freedom, cf. Wild, *Introduction to Realistic Philosophy* (New York: Harper, 1948), chaps. ii–iv.

[17] Cf. M. Heidegger, *Vom Wesen des Grundes* (Frankfurt am Main: Klostermann, 1954–56).

ments. This conception has had a wide influence, and is now threatening the very existence of authentic freedom. It rests on a misconception of that basic horizon of freedom which underlies not only human thought and action but the human world as such.

Christianity and humanism are allied in opposing this confusion of freedom with license, and this alliance has saved the traces of freedom which still remain in our Western culture. But the Christian view recognizes the radical scope of freedom, and differs from classical humanism in the following respects. It rests on a far more somber view of man and his situation in history. The world is not a chaos, and glimpses of order can be observed, which suggest certain moral laws. Our reason is very human. But even if he knows, man cannot act in accordance with this knowledge. He is weighed down by too great a burden of past confusion and sin, which penetrates not only into his passions but into every phase of his existence, including the intelligence. He can be freed from this burden only by forgiveness coming from a source that is wholly independent and transcendent. He may then become free for a sacrifice of his self-centered world, and for a new life of obedience in a new world ordered to a different center. This life, however, involves a constant struggle. There is no assurance that it will be granted security or self-realization in the flux of earthly history.

b. The coming of reason brought with it this course of history.[18] But for the rational mode of reflection and speculation that began in ancient Greece, the capricious contingencies of this history have been a constant embarrassment and even scandal. Reason has always tried to escape from them to a spectatorial position outside the world. From this unbiased position it has hoped to gain an objective view of the

---

[18] For a penetrating consideration of the relation between rationalism and history, cf. Gusdorf, *Mythe et métaphysique,* Part II, especially chap i.

facts of life and history, and then to enclose them within
a single system of timeless truth. We are now witnessing the
last expression of this rationalistic hope in the many philosophies of history which have been produced by recent authors.
These attempts to squeeze history into a fixed framework
and to grasp its final meaning have failed. Instead of a single
reason, we find many rational systems, each relative to the
thought of the time and the interests of the author. So, behind a vaunted display of necessity, we are brought back to
an underlying contingency. Instead of history being included
within the framework of a single rational system, we find
many rational systems included within the ultimate horizon
of world history.

In Christianity we find a very different attitude toward
this horizon, for it is itself founded on historic events, and
is conscious of itself as a historic phenomenon. Hence when
left to itself, it makes no claim to a timeless truth or to any
position within the reach of man which is outside human
history. In all such claims it sees a pretentious divinizing of
man condemned by St. Paul as the foolishness of the Greeks.
One can have faith in the meaning of history. But the final
meaning of this vast outpouring of contingent events and
interpretations will never be coherently understood and
explained by a human mind that is still living within it.
This meaning is eschatological. It will not be given before
the end, and will be given, when it is given, by God, and
not by man.

c. Rationalism thinks of man as a substance living within
an external, cosmic order not essentially involved in his
being. Thus his thoughts and choices go on inside him, and
have no effect on the objective universe. In this sense, he
is cut off from the world, or in other words, the whole world
phenomenon, which is relative to man, is missing. Similar
cuts are also made in man understood subjectively. Thus,
as we have noted, the divine reason in man is sharply sepa-

rated from sensation, desire, and the other human faculties, as they were called.

These artificial cuts are absent from the Biblical anthropology and from Christian thought that has managed to resist rationalist influences coming from the surrounding culture. When it is said of Christ in the Gospel of John that *he came into the world and the world received him not,* this does not mean an objective universe of science, but the concrete world in which men live that is relative to their being. Man and his world belong together, and our basic interpretations and choices affect the world in which we live. This insight is also found in the Pauline Epistles.[19] Furthermore no dualistic splits are recognized in human nature. The reason in us is not divine. It is very human, and is just as seriously affected by historical guilt and corruption as the other aspects of our nature. The human individual with his body, mind, spirit, and his world exist together in one integral structure no part of which can be without the others.

d. From the objective point of view of reason, however, this individual world is largely invisible. Hence it is readily ignored and discounted as internal and subjective. The social world of the group, on the other hand, with the co-operative agencies and products of technology, is objective and visible. Hence this objective, social world cannot be ignored. For a long time, rational philosophy identified it with the cosmic order of nature, and regarded political rulers as natural powers that must simply be accepted, like sun, and sea, and storm. Even when, in modern times, this was recognized as a human phenomenon, the priority of the group over the individual was still maintained with special clarity in such influential philosophies as those of Hegel and Marx. It is typical of rational reflection to regard the individual as a smaller part of the larger, objective group, to minimize his

[19] Cf. Bultmann, *Theology of the New Testament,* I, 254–259.

basic freedom, and to subject him to those utilitarian principles of self-realization and survival which govern all objective behavior.

Christian faith offers us an entirely different approach. The original revelation is accomplished in the life of an individual person, Jesus. He is in his own person the sign of the times for which his generation is looking. He does not bring an impersonal set of laws, but a personal message coming from himself to other persons. Hence the antitheses of the Sermon on the Mount: "You have heard that it was said of the men of old. . . . But I say to you . . ." This message is directed primarily to the free person, and calls him to decision.[20] The social effects come later. Thus the parables of the leaven and the mustard seed point to the large, social results which may emerge from minute, individual beginnings.

It is true that from an objective and static point of view, the group is prior to the individual, and includes him as a part. But we must not forget that if the group is to remain alive, its purposes must be first understood and loved by the individual. Thus from an existential and dynamic point of view, the individual is prior to the group. It is in his mind and heart that new purposes are born. A Christian society is like the course of a comet in which a small luminous head leads the way, and the great expanse of the tail follows after. There is an eternal dimension in personal existence. Resurrection is promised to the individual, not to the group. Hence authentic Christian faith always brings with it a deeper respect for the potentialities of the individual person, the sense of a less restricted freedom, and a new kind of ethics about which we must now say a few words (cf. Chapter VI).

e. This new mode of existence is centered not around the self or the human society, but toward something tran-

[20] *Ibid.,* I, 13.

scendent, and is beyond general rules and laws. Instead of obedience to a principle, for which credit is claimed, we find here obedience to a spirit of love and devotion for which no credit is claimed. Instead of the imposition of law on a unique situation by deliberation and casuistry, we find a free person meeting it by generosity and love.

We call this, of course, the Christian ethic, and think of it as a theological ideal expressed, but usually not followed, by Christians in the Church. It is true, indeed, that such conduct is rarely seen anywhere, but the ideal is recognized in secular life far beyond the limits of what we call the Christian Church. The notions of generosity, forgiveness,[21] and sacrifice are found generally in the East as well as the West, and such action when recognized, even in imperfect forms, in living individuals is universally admired.

It would seem that Christianity has sharply focused, cultivated, and sometimes exemplified in personal action a way of existing that is an essential possibility always latent in personal freedom. Is it latent in the human group? History tells us of individuals who really sacrificed themselves, who gave up their lives for something transcending them. Does it tell us of group sacrifices that are really equivalent? Can a human empire or state be expected to act in accordance with the Christian ethic? Would such action actually be right? We shall later (Chapters VII and VIII) turn to these questions which must be faced by any Christian philosophy. But before this, we must attempt to clarify what we mean by a Christian philosophy, and the way in which it must now meet the age-old issues between "reason" and "faith."

[21] Cf. A. Martin, "A Realistic Theory of Forgiveness," in *The Return to Reason*, ed. J. Wild (Chicago: Regnery, 1953), pp. 313 ff.

Chapter Three

CHRISTIAN HISTORY: THE CONFUSION OF REASON WITH FAITH

In the first chapter we examined the transition from mythical society to historical culture and that rational way of thought and life which, for Plato and his successors, was exemplified in the free, individual person of Socrates. We pointed out how the primitive culture grasps the whole of its life together in a mythical mode of understanding which is based on a feeling for transcendence, and in other ways resembles what we now call religion. In one respect, however, the two are quite different. The global myth pervades every phase of primitive life and orders them all into a single life-world in such a way that, as we said, the whole of life becomes a many-sided liturgy. With the coming of the free person who is able to interpret the world for himself, this global structure breaks down, and each basic phase of the cultural endeavor, like trade and politics, now emerges as something distinct from the rest with a certain autonomy of its own.

Folk songs and recitations, which once expressed the mythical apprehension of the whole community, gradually become musical and poetic objects, heard and interpreted by different individuals in different ways. Re-enactments of the myth and expressive dances lose their liturgical significance, and are now put on a stage, where they are objectively regarded by a detached audience which participates only aesthetically or in a partial, objective way. The global myth, once pervading the whole life of the community, is now restricted to a special province of the sacred, and handed over to the special care of a priestly caste. Also, as we have seen, a formidable rival now looms on the scene, the gnostic quest of philosophy for an objective and critical understanding of God, the world, and man. This approach gives us a certain objective perspective on things, which, within certain limits, can be intersubjectively verified with the aid of the human senses.

However, it cannot help us to understand the *Lebenswelt* in its totality and, more especially, individual existence as it is lived from the inside, and the mystery under which it can be grasped together as one. These basic factors of the *Lebenswelt* have been handed over to religion. So a fundamental opposition now emerges which has dominated our intellectual history ever since. On the one hand, we have the rational enterprise of philosophy which alone is supposed to be able to attain universal agreement through rational argument concerning fixed objective truth, but which abstracts from the concrete life-world and is blind to subjectivity and transcendence. On the other, we have religion, which is close to the life-world and the mystery which envelops it, but has no part in reason and objective, universal truth. The free individual of our Western history no longer has access to a global myth that can encompass his world as a whole. These two alternatives, faith and reason as they are still called, confront him. He may either choose one or the other, or attempt to find a synthesis. During the greater part of our history the latter has prevailed, and time after time we have been presented with systems which claim to bring the two together.

To write the history of these attempts in detail would be to write the history of Western thought. We have no time for this. Nevertheless, we may be able to select certain critical examples by which we may gain an understanding of three important types of synthesis, all of which now have broken down. The first is the classic type of intellectualism found in Plato and Aristotle. The second is the dialectical type which came only after Christianity, and is found in Augustine and Hegel. Finally (third), there is the dogmatic type of faith supremacy which is found in the medieval synthesis of St. Thomas Aquinas. After a brief review of these three "solutions" and of the reasons for their decline, we shall turn to our own situation at the present time, where we find the two in separation. After a critical study of this unstable situation, we shall make certain suggestions concerning what we may learn from this history and a further possibility toward which it clearly points.

1. *Greek Intellectualism: Plato and Aristotle*

Let us first examine the view, deeply ingrained in our tradition, that would definitely subordinate personal faith and the concrete world of human existence to the objective universe of reason. On this view, faith has no world of its own. It is a purely individual or "subjective" commitment that occurs within a fixed cosmic order, and cannot be successfully realized unless it adjusts to this independent order which transcends and envelops it. Values are objective beings or properties. Lower values can be grasped by sense; higher ones by reason alone. The moral life is a constant struggle between voluntary tendencies elicited by reason and material appetites elicited by sense. The supreme value is a being higher than all others, the first cause, endowed with an array of attributes analogous to those found in man but freed from all imperfection, and intensified to the highest degree. This divine being is thus inclusive of all perfection, absolutely undivided or simple, absolutely good, absolutely intelligent and omniscient, absolutely powerful, completely timeless and eternal.

Many different versions of this rational absolute have been constructed in the history of Western thought. But they all resemble one another in being all-inclusive, timeless, impersonal, and rational to a supereminent degree. The absolute being has established an order of lesser beings, or degrees of being, which corresponds to a value scale. The closer we are to the absolute, the higher we are in value. Thus power is better than impotence, and reason better than the irrational. The practical life of man takes place within this fixed order, and is usually guided by opinion or faith, a view that is blurred and distorted by the particular circumstances, and incidental history of the individual in question. Self-realization is the final good for man. This can be achieved only by first clarifying opinion through rational insight, and then by regulating desire in accordance with the order thus revealed.

This view originated in ancient Greece. It is poignantly expressed in Plato's famous image of the Cave, wherein the human life-world is compared to a gloomy, underground cavern, and concrete experience to a fleeting succession of shadows. Men are advised to leave this realm of opinion or faith, and to climb up into vaster regions where things can be seen as they really are in the light of the sun by the divine reason dwelling within us. Here the historical life-world is included within the fixed cosmos, the subjective within the objective, and faith, or opinion, definitely subordinated to reason. Aristotle gives another more abstract expression of the same view in the Sixth Book of his *Nicomachean Ethics* (Chapter VII) where he argues for the supremacy of pure theoretical wisdom (*sophia*) over practical insight (*phronesis*). The distinctive nature of each species gives it a biased perspective on things relative to its special needs. What is good for a rabbit is not good for a fish. Hence practical insight varies from species to species.

Man is no exception to this reign of subjectivity. He also lives in a special world perspective that is relative to his needs. The practical know-how that guides his life is not like that of a fish. But he also has access to another higher wisdom (*sophia*) which is not relative to any special, human trait. Such knowledge is purely objective and impartial. Hence if any other species of being possessed this divine faculty, its abstract, theoretical knowledge would be precisely the same, for it reflects the being of each thing not as it is in relation to some other but as it is in itself. Man can achieve such objective knowledge, and it is only in its light that he can gain some clear, unbiased understanding of the supreme being and of his highest good.

Only when his relative practical opinions are illumined by this higher insight can it achieve the highest excellence. Thus the relative life-world is included within the universe, and *phronesis* (faith) is subordinated to *sophia* (reason). This classical rationalism is foreign to Hebrew and Christian thought. But, as we shall see, it was worked out in a special way in the Middle Ages, and was given varying expressions in modern times by such thinkers as Spinoza, Leibnitz, and Hegel. Since faith and reason are quite different, confusion is bound to arise if they are simply mixed together. Hence the effort to fit them into a natural order, in which each can perform its distinctive functions, represents an important advance. Nevertheless the rationalistic attempt to defend the subordination of the world of faith to its objective universe faces serious objections. We shall consider the general question of world priority more thoroughly in a later chapter (V). At this point, we shall suggest a few major objections to this basic thesis of Western rationalism by using the revealing symbols of Plato's classic image of the Cave. In the first place, we may doubt whether the objective universe is in any sense prior to the human life-world and independent of it. This idea fails to fit the facts of social and individual history. Man existed in the concrete world for many millennia before the appearance of rational reflection and science. Furthermore, the human thinker must grow up in the everyday world before he becomes a philosopher or scientist. Lost in his investigations of what he calls other regions, and even other worlds, he may forget when and where he is. But actually his theories belong to human history, and he remains in the same moving world as the rest of us. Science begins in the *Lebenswelt*, proceeds in a special region within it, and ends by being purposefully used to transform it. If we were to give a picture of *these* facts in terms of Plato's famous myth, we would have to invert the image.

The world that is already there in the first place is not the underground cavern but the vast upper region where men work and struggle out of doors in the light of the sun. It is here that human life and history begins. Rational thinkers and scientists are a special group of men. In this respect Plato was right. But they do not climb up. They descend into a gloomy, cavernous region of their own, more adapted to the weakness of their eyes. Here they build a fire which they can look at directly, and simulate the conditions of the upper world. Taking various things down into their Cave, they examine them one by one, paying no attention to their color and resistance, and making no use of them at all. As scientists they simply regard the shadows cast on the wall, and how different successions of shadows correspond to different manipulations of things. Strangely enough, this objective information, which started as a mere game, turns out to be very useful in the upper world where luminous things, put together in various ways, continue to produce the luminous results that can be predicted from watching the order of shadows.

Hence, as time goes on, more and more people descend to the caves which are widened and extended. Then, as Plato points out, since the sun hurts their eyes, many prefer to remain underground. Living comfortably on mushrooms, snails, and manufactured articles, they claim that their cavern, now vast in size, is the real world after all. Going up is hardly worth while, for this is only a secondary and derivative region of headaches where all is confused, except in the dusk, and where no one can ever see anything definite clearly. At this juncture, the incident told by Plato might well take place. Only he left out the earlier history which slightly alters the meaning, for meanings grow and develop in history. It is by no means clear that the objective universe of science is prior to the *Lebenswelt*. This is a first fundamental doubt.

In the second place, we may wonder whether it is really richer and more inclusive. Is it not clear that science depends on special methods and operations? Is it not abstract, and does it not, therefore, necessarily omit certain factors that are present in the life-world? In truth, there are such factors. Later on we shall return to them for a fuller consideration. At this point, we shall refer to them only briefly, using the imagery of Plato's myth to suggest their presence in the concrete horizon of everyday existence.

There are terms like being, everything, the whole world, which seem to be all-inclusive in scope, and for which the claim is made that they correspond to concepts with rational meaning. But this claim is open to question. Such terms also belong to ordinary discourse, and centuries of rational speculation have failed to bring out any clear-cut rational meaning. *Being* now means no more to a trained philosopher than the confused and hazy sense it carries in the everyday language of the *Lebenswelt*. We need not infer that such a prethematic sense is not present, or that it cannot be developed and in a certain way "clarified." But we should infer that this sense is not wholly rational, and that it will never be clarified by the normal procedures of objective science. This is because what we call "reason" is always abstract and partial. We can examine things impartially and objectively only one by one.

Each genuine science has its own special point of view which enables it to grasp a certain kind of being and to omit the rest. Thus geometry examines things so far as they are extended; physics, things as extended and moving; and biology, things as living. Other sciences study one thing or one set of things, ignoring the rest, as geology studies the earth, and astronomy the stars. There is no science of everything.

The rationalist will conclude that such a term (everything) is therefore meaningless. But he will be wrong, for meanings are not exclusively rational. Such a term refers not to any scientific perspective in an abstract way, but rather to the prescientific horizon of the *Lebenswelt* where the data of the different sciences are never neatly separated but where, as we say, everything happens together at once. This word cannot be exactly and objectively defined. Nevertheless we all know what it means in a prethematic way from our life in the *Lebenswelt,* and our lived participation in its history. This horizon may be more confused. But it is certainly more inclusive. Hence in terms of Plato's image, it is evidently the real, upper world where stars, mountains, flowing streams, verdant pastures, wolves, human beings, and their temples are all found together in darkness and shadow, or gleaming in the light of the sun. This is the prior and wider horizon.

On this point, Plato made a mistake from which the West has not yet recovered. The universe of science does not encompass and precede the world of life. It is rather the concrete world of human existence from which science takes its origin, and in which it lives and has its being. In terms of the analogy, science, with its abstract perspectives and its technical vocabulary, ever burrowing deeper into its special objects by means of special manipulations expressed in unfamiliar and technical language, is precisely the region of the underground cave. This cave has its own advantages. Here we make a light of our own in whose dimness we can "clearly" analyze the shadow cast by each real thing and the shadows resulting from our manipulations. All this is clear and precise and very useful. But the cave cannot include the upper world. Many factors are missing, the most evident being the concrete togetherness, called *confusion,* of *everything* in the real world. But two other factors (3 and 4) are also strikingly absent, and to these we must now turn.

The third is the bias or concern of subjectivity and the direct inner feeling of this history. The upper world is wide and rich, offering many possibilities for diverse ways of life and understanding. Here real choices must be made. Some choose to stand the pain of the sun, to climb into the mountain peaks, and watch the world by day. Others sleep in the day, wandering through the twilight forests, and watching the moon and stars by night. Still others go underground to build their own fires and live in the shadowy caves. Each choice is correlated with a way of seeing. Furthermore these inhabitants of the upper world are not merely aware of objects. They also have a sense of their own subjectivity.

Thus the cave dweller in Plato's story, released from his chains, must turn himself around and move himself from within. He does not merely watch this revolution of his being from the outside, but feels it directly from within. As he first tries to look at genuinely luminous objects, he suffers pain in the eyes and anxiety at the unaccustomed spectacle. So he may return to the objects with which he is familiar. Or he may decide to accept inner pain and confusion, and to climb up into the world of struggle and light. If he does so, new alternatives will confront him. In this open world, he must keep moving and choosing, for even to stay in the open requires a constantly repeated choice. And if he decides to return to the closed world of the cavern, this also is a choice. Furthermore, his successive experiences are held together by this subjective awareness. He remembers the choices he has made, and the diverse possibilities to which they lead. Life in the open world is not only objective but subjectively centered. In other words, it is a history. Let us now contrast this with the other life enclosed in the Cave.

As we have pointed out, this is also a history, for the prisoners have decided to enclose themselves. But once in the nether region, they see for the most part only reflected shadows on the wall. These shadowy shapes can be easily seen with no trouble, and the order of their succession carefully noted and remembered. This is called clarity and exactitude. In watching this play of reflections, the observers must remain in a fixed position between the wall and the fire. If they get too close to the screen, their own shadow will interfere, and even if they move their heads, the vision will be blurred. So, as Plato himself says, their necks must be chained in a fixed position. This attitude, in fact, is called objectivity and impartiality. Any self-motion which upsets the shadow play is an unwelcome, subjective intrusion. Of course all motion and feeling cannot be avoided. But the prisoners, when advanced in cave-life, identify themselves with their shadows. This is what they really are, and any denial of this is a vestige of infantile confusion. Their own shadows are not unlike the shadows of things, and seem to succeed each other in regular ways. So why exaggerate the difference?

The observer himself casts a shadow, as also even the screen. So the time will come when eventually, through a complicated arrangement of screens reflecting into other screens, and recording of micro-films, every possible motion of man or thing will be objectively recorded and fitted into regular laws of succession on which valid predictions may be based. Under these conditions, free action and self-consciousness are discouraged. An irregular, unexpected motion is inconvenient. To give way to inner feeling is to indulge in sheer subjectivity, and to leave the company of rational men. It is better to gaze at the shadow succession it casts on the screen, or if none as yet can be seen, to imagine what it would be like, and to devise a set of screens delicate enough to catch it as it really is.

Hence very few choices are made, and the sense of subjectivity is suppressed. Life is no longer held together by an active subjective center. This is discounted as partial and biased. It is rather enclosed within the supposedly limitless horizon of a fixed, objective screen. What cannot be clearly reflected on this is mere confusion, and does not really exist. Everything but this confusion can be reflected on some screen. And this is no loss. Human existence abandons its subjective center. History is reduced to the succession of historic facts. Man loses himself in his shadows. He tries to detach himself from himself, and vanishes in objective reflections.

The fourth factor is that of transcendence and value, symbolized in the image by the sun and color. As Plato points out, the creative source of value (the sun) shines directly only in the upper world. But it is completely transcendent, for no one looks directly at the sun. Nevertheless we can move toward it or away from it as we choose. And on this choice will depend the meaning (light) which orders and pervades our view of the world, and the values (colors) by which we live and act. These meanings and values radiate from a transcendent source that is glimpsed only in the *Lebenswelt*. But they can be received in a vast variety of ways, and each individual is free not only to choose which values he will pursue, but how and even whether he is to pursue them. He is responsible for his view, and the world in which he lives is his own, even if he retires from the light and descends to the caves.

The sunlight never penetrates into the caverns. Here there is no direct sense of transcendence. The sun is not reflected on any screen. It casts no shadow whatsoever, or as is said in cave language, transcendence is not a fact. Instead of this, men build feeble fires of their own, and thus regard themselves as the real authors of meaning and value so far as these terms are understood, which is only very dimly. The light is so hazy that it is hard to distinguish it from darkness (meaninglessness) and meaning is confused with objects bearing meaning. Thus being is confused with beings, and time with successive events in time. Colors (values) also fail to stand out, and merge with their dusky background. On the screen they are not reflected at all, and this is held to be an advantage. In cave language it is said: *science is neutral to value.* The colors are hard to look at in direct firelight. So this is in general discouraged. They are accepted for the time being as an unfortunate necessity now purely subjective, since they cast no real shadow. But it is hoped that in the future, by some new device, they may be reflected as different successions of shadows on color film, and thus more clearly understood. Those who believe the tales about the sun in the upper world imagine it in anthropomorphic terms as a big fire in the sky, and think about it objectively as a shadowless spot on the screen, though of course it is no object.

It would be interesting, and perhaps illuminating, to develop further the possibilities of this suggestive image. At this point, however, we must stop. We hope that by our inverted interpretation, which is certainly not inappropriate to the image, we may have been able to suggest to the reader certain critical difficulties standing in the way of Plato's intellectualistic interpretation which has exerted such a profound influence on the history of Western thought. According to this view, the faith that guides our existence in the *Lebenswelt* is subordinate to objective reason, and the life-world itself is included in the objective universe of science. We have used Plato's image to show that such a position is untenable, because any objective universe, no matter how vast in scope, must lack certain factors, concrete togetherness, subjective choice and history, global meaning, value, and transcendence which belong to the *Lebenswelt*. Hence what we call *reason* is a derived perspective on things that grows out of this prior world, and *reason* presupposes faith.

In terms of Aristotle's argument, we can say that individuals, and even species, with different living faiths may come to agree on an abstract, rational perspective. But the idea that such a perspective can include each individual, and each species, as it exists and lives in itself is a great delusion, the delusion of all rationalism. What we grasp in this way is not existence as it is lived but only objective shadows of this existence. The thing itself cannot be derived from its shadow, but the shadow from the existing thing. Reason puts itself forth as a floating view that is everywhere and nowhere with no real point of origin. But this is a figment without foundation. Reason will not be exercised except by someone who exists somewhere, who has faith in it, and so chooses. Reason can never comprehend this existence which it presupposes. It can never be the guide for faith and freedom.

So why not admit that the two are strictly different, that neither one can absorb or include the other? Let us try rather to combine them in a higher synthesis to which each makes a real contribution. This alternative has appealed to great thinkers in our history, and has exerted a widespread influence. So let us now examine it.

2. The Combining of Faith and Reason: St. Augustine and Hegel

There is something very sound in the urge to bring faith together with reason. This is, in fact, a basic need of our time, for which Christian philosophy may provide an answer. But if we examine the many historical attempts which have been made to achieve such a synthesis, we cannot help but be impressed by the serious obstacles that stand in the way. The most serious of these is the sharp difference and even opposition between the two. Faith involves us in a transcendent mystery from which we cannot remain detached, and where we are no longer the masters but must submit. Of course this revelation of mystery must be humanly understood and assimilated. But faith has its own ways of understanding. These are quite different from those of reason which involves us only in problems. From these problems we can remain detached, and for them we may hope to discover fixed "solutions." As we have noted, the one seems to be governed by a spirit of obedience, the other by a spirit of freedom, and it is hard to see how these can be united without destroying the autonomy of one at least, or perhaps of both together. Our Western history, in fact, offers us many examples of such onesided unions.

The Augustinian (Anselmian) formula, *fides quaerens intellectum*, represents a great attempt to combine faith and reason on a more or less equal footing from which we can still learn much. The impossibility of escaping from prior value judgments and choices is clearly recognized. These prior commitments, which underlie all demonstration, cannot themselves be rationally demonstrated, and to them is allotted the guiding role. The first step must be a vague hypothesis, an act of faith. But this is only a beginning. The vagueness and darkness of faith must be corrected so far as this is possible. Here lies the task of reason which alone can provide us with clear insight. This profound conception not only sees the need of one factor for the other, but also their profound antagonism. Thus after initiating the process of understanding, faith is asked to commit suicide, and reason finally destroys the very ladder on which it climbs. This dialectical conception is, indeed, profound. But it rests on a certain misconception which has led to serious errors and confusions.

The initial acts of faith are not rational hypotheses or propositions subject to proof or disproof by objective evidence. They belong to an entirely different world of existence and truth. Hence the objective analyst rightly complains that they are unfalsifiable in any of the normal ways familiar to him. They are not propositions of science. They belong to a different order, the order of faith. Hence the idea that they can directly assist the investigation of science, and can be eventually replaced by objective insights of reason is a delusion inherited from Greek rationalism. This delusion has brought forth many vain attempts of reason to achieve the impossible, and to accomplish what has been called a clear and thorough rationalization of the faith, like Anselm's *a priori* proof of the existence of God and his demonstration of the rational necessity of the Incarnation. In this way Augustinianism has often led to an overweening rationalism which is incompatible with the autonomy of faith.

But these attempts finally failed, and with faith refusing to commit suicide, the Augustinian tradition in the long run fell into an opposite emphasis on the guiding function of faith which was incompatible with the autonomy of reason. This faith became rigidly crystallized, and lost touch with the world of the twelfth century. Granting philosophy no right to form its own hypotheses, it could not meet the challenge of Aristotelian naturalism which filtered into Europe about the year 1200, and broke down in the thirteenth century. Philosophy has its own evidence, its own methods, and its own freedom. And when this is interfered with, philosophy will rightly resist.

But the existential world of faith also possesses its own evidence and its own autonomy, and rightly resists the attempts of philosophy to absorb it into closed, objective systems, the greatest of which was that of Hegel. Here human existence and Christian faith are both absorbed into a dialectical panorama of world history. But this great system has been unable to meet the challenge of its keenest critics, Marx and Kierkegaard, each of whom in his own way pointed out the incapacity of objective reason to do justice to life as it is lived in the concrete, and to a living faith. Hence the Hegelian system broke down and failed to survive the nineteenth century. It is true, indeed, that faith should be combined with reason, but only in such a way as to maintain each in its own proper autonomy. Augustinianism in the long run failed to find room for philosophic freedom, while Hegelianism failed with respect to the autonomy of faith.

There are, of course, many instances of eclectic syntheses, philosophy standing by the side of faith. But we need not dwell on these. There is a world of faith and a realm of reason. Both of them are dynamic manifestations of life which cannot be confused with their dead deposits. Hence to combine them must mean a living interaction of some kind. How can this be achieved in some integral manner without reducing one to the other? Perhaps we have been mistaken in ignoring a certain hierarchical order that holds between the two. Perhaps each has an independent function to perform in its own way, but one in natural subordination to the other. The intellectualist holds that faith should be subordinated to reason. But history has failed to sustain this solution. There is another possibility. Why should not reason be ancillary to faith as was widely held in the Middle Ages? Let us now examine this alternative.

3. *Reason Subordinate to Faith: The Thomist Synthesis*

In the Jewish-Christian tradition we find a mode of thought which is not so much concerned with developing an objective perspective on things as with revealing the character of personal existence in the life-world. This world is open to transcendence, and the Biblical literature does not present us with a set of theories about nature and man but rather with the history of a meeting between man and an awesome mystery, not envisaged as an object but actively encountered by faith as the living God. This difference is evident in the very style of the writings which avoids the detached, technical language of science, and employs the expressive, ordinary language of the *Lebenswelt*. Such language can be grasped only by an understanding that is aware of its own existence and actively engaged. This active understanding, so far as it becomes involved in the encounter with transcendence, is what is known as faith. For anyone thus involved, it must take precedence over all other concerns, including science and philosophy.

Hence in the great medieval synthesis which attempted to bring Greek wisdom together with religion, reason is subordinate to faith. In view of its central importance in our Western history, let us now examine this synthesis with the following questions in mind. Is what is called *reason* here the same as human philosophy? Does this synthesis make room for the genuine autonomy of philosophy? Does it do full justice to Christian faith? Does it avoid the dangers of separation and confusion which our analysis has already revealed? In order to answer these questions, we must first briefly remind ourselves of the major concepts and doctrines underlying this synthesis as it is presented in the system of Aquinas.

The conception of reason is taken directly from Greek thought. Reason is, indeed, a faculty of the human soul which cannot be brought into operation without the aid of the senses. But in itself it is detached from the physical nature of the rational individual, and its proper acts are immaterial. At the beginning, it is absolutely empty and indeterminate, which separates it from the determinate limits of its bearer. Because of this emptiness, it is unlimited in scope, and able to assimilate the specific forms and natures of all things whatsoever, including that of its human host. It has no subjective understanding of itself in act, for this would indentify it with a particular process in time. It must wait for itself to happen and then, from a detached point of view, apprehend this past act as an object before itself. The mind can never identify itself strictly with any particular existence. If so, it would lose its independence, which rests upon detachment. Hence it identifies itself only formally and objectively with every thing that it knows, being one with the essence of the thing but remaining detached from its act of existing. By this objective knowledge it attains a timeless truth concerning the fixed hierarchy of beings which constitute the universe, inorganic things, plants, animals, men, angels, and the eternal first mover, God.

Man has nothing to do with the constitution of this universe. To regard things from his own, or even from a human point of view, is to fall into error and distortion. His supreme, natural function is to know it exactly as it is in itself, and then to adjust himself to it, as it is already and ever must be, by intelligent or virtuous action. Only in this way will he realize his fixed natural end of happiness. The reason which enables him to do this is something more than human. It is immaterial and lacking any finite determination. Hence it is something divine, in fact, *the divine image in man.* The science of metaphysics, or theology, which enables him to know something of being and its necessary laws, the cosmic order as a whole, and to prove the existence of God and His necessary attributes, is a *divine science.* This supreme, objective knowledge, and the different special sciences that follow in its train, are timelessly true. It is philosophy itself, a human participation in the eternal knowledge of God. Any deviation from it is an error. It is not a point of view but a vision of the truth itself, the one and only valid and perennial philosophy. Is it reasonable to accept this last proposition?

If there is one kind of knowledge not covered by this account, or one kind of evidence conspicuously omitted, serious doubt will be cast on this claim. We shall now briefly mention one kind of knowledge and one kind of evidence to which we have already referred, and with which all men are familiar, to justify this doubt. There is such knowledge and evidence. It is true that men are aware of objects. But they also have a direct awareness of their own existence in the very act. I know the movement of my hand within the hand as I am moving it. Unless I had such knowledge in fact, the notion of object would lose its meaning—the non-subjective which depends upon this contrast. I know my own existence directly in its act. Such knowledge is not clearly recognized in the Thomistic synthesis, and this omission is fraught with many consequences.

My acts are not enclosed within a subjective container. They are intentionally stretched out toward objects of various kinds to the farthest limits of the world, and in religious devotion to something transcending it. This horizon is subjective as well as objective, and can be understood only by following our intentions through from their personal center to their ultimate objects. This is the world of history in which we live and exist. When this ultimate horizon is regarded externally from a detached point of view, it is reduced and distorted. Subjective concern and transcendence are simply omitted, and the world horizon is placed within an alien frame. The living subject is objectified. Instead of existence we have essence; instead of first personal concern we have mere objects in motion; and instead of history a succession of events in time.

We shall return to this final horizon of the *Lebenswelt* in a later chapter (V). At present we must be content with this brief reference, and with the further remark that it is not adequately developed or even clearly recognized in the Thomistic synthesis. This should suffice to show that its claim to be the perennial philosophy is unjustified. It is one philosophical point of view among many. It presents us with an objective perspective on things in the *Lebenswelt*. But such a perspective is always derived and posterior. Like the various perspectives of science with which it is closely allied, it grows out of history in the life-world. But it is unable to illumine and to interpret the concrete existence of human persons in this ultimate horizon. Far from being the definitive philosophy, it is a philosophical perspective inadequately aware of its own limitations, and, therefore, subject to grave errors and distortions.

Let us now turn to the second question—does this synthesis make room for the genuine autonomy of philosophy? The answer has to be *No*. This is because it fails to recognize the ambiguity of the human situation, and the freedom of the human mind to develop different global interpretations of the available evidence. This freedom is very evident not only in the different world-views of different cultures but in the history of Western philosophy. In this history we find not merely different theories within a fixed objective frame, but different interpretations of the frame itself, divergent structures of meaning. These different views of the world cannot be squeezed into a single frame without arbitrary violence and neglect. Thomistic thought, of course, has a place for freedom within the cosmic order, but global world meanings are held to be passively assimilated by an empty mind. Hence there is no room for basic choices affecting the very order of the world in which we live. But the history of Western thought is an expression of such freedom. It presents us with basic choices of precisely this global kind.

The claim of Greek rationalism to be the one and only perennial philosophy has led it to condemn other approaches arbitrarily as fallacious and heretical, though they are equally well grounded on the available philosophical evidence. More particularly it has rejected approaches more closely allied with the dynamic, historical character of Hebrew thought as subjective and relativistic. This has prevented it from exploring the nature of lived experience and from interpreting the human *Lebenswelt*. It has accepted the doctrine that truth is one, and has often construed this doctrine in an univocal sense which has blinded it to the richness of being and other orders of truth, such as religious truth, scientific truth, and aesthetic truth which are radically different in structure. In terms of this narrow conception, it has defended the right of theology to exercise a certain veto power over philosophy, otherwise held to be completely autonomous. The philosopher must, of course, express the truth as it is given to him in evidence that is accessible to all men. But if he makes any statement that contradicts a proposition in revealed theology, he must be wrong, since truth is one. It is hard to see how this right of veto can be defended against the charge of a dogmatic restriction on the freedom of philosophy. Also it raises serious questions concerning the nature of religious truth and its expression in objective propositions to which we must now turn.

Can authentic faith be adequately expressed in terms of such articles or propositions? Does this traditional conception actually do justice to the distinctive character of living faith? Here again our answer must be *No,* because of certain differences to which we shall now only briefly refer.

Thomism holds that articles of faith do not differ from rational propositions except that they are affirmed not on the basis of adequate evidence but rather by an act of will on the basis of unimpeachable authority. Like all opinion, they are a weak form of knowledge whose premises cannot be demonstrated. Once accepted by the will, however, they must be developed and ordered by the usual methods of logic. A proposition is about some object which is regarded within a frame of detached, mental vision. It is true or false, depending on its agreement or disagreement with some fact distinct from itself, and this can be decided on the basis of an examination of the object or objects in question. Hence the propositional attitude is impersonal and abstracts, so far as possible, from the subjective attitude of him who is asserting it. From this point of view, it makes no difference whether he is concerned with it or wholly indifferent. His attitude and even his assertion of the proposition are mere instruments for finding the objective truth. Once the truth of a proposition has been established, it may be used, with other true propositions, to deduce further truths with which it may be finally combined to form a logical system covering its proper field.

Faith cannot be reduced to a propositional system of this sort without radical reduction and distortion. My faith is not *about* any object, but *in* a person or *in* something closely involved with personal existence whether it be subpersonal or transcendent. Thus we say that a man has faith *in* himself, *in* some project to which he has become deeply committed like the United Nations, for example, or *in* God. Faith can be examined and criticized but never from a detached and impersonal point of view. A person who looks at his faith in this way is either in the process of losing it, or is confusing it with something else. Hence the notorious powerlessness of rational arguments for the existence of God, and the basic ineffectiveness of religious "argument" in general. This is because my faith involves my whole being in its ultimate direction, so that I cannot get outside it to place it in an objective frame. To frame any living faith is to kill it. It can be understood not within any special perspective but only within the ultimate horizon of the *Lebenswelt* itself, where it arises from personal choice.

Hence the truth of faith is not a matter of agreement between some proposition and an objective fact. It is subjective as well as objective, and depends upon the intensity and certainty with which it is held. No one would refer to a vague and lackadaisical concern as an example of true faith. Such an attitude has its coherent unity which cannot be broken down into independent propositions or articles. But it is certainly not a rational system, and while the relations of its various parts can be understood in the light of the whole, they cannot be understood by logical calculation or deduction. Faith has its own mode of knowing, and its own ways of deepening and reflecting on itself. These comments may suffice to show that grave questions may be raised as to whether the Thomistic doctrine of the articles of faith, and the objective logic it uses in the development of its dogmatic theology really do justice to the structure of any living faith, including its own.

This tradition has exercised a guiding role throughout long periods of our history. It claims to stand for the supremacy of living faith over philosophy and the whole of human existence in the world. In the light of our investigations, this seems to be a last alternative. As we have suggested, no authentic justification can be given for the separation of faith from philosophy, for the confusion of one with the other, or for the subordination of faith to so-called reason, the ideal of wisdom in ancient Greece. Is this claim of the great medieval synthesis then to be accepted? Has it avoided these erroneous alternatives? Does it actually represent the subordination of genuine philosophy to genuine faith? A brief examination can now tell us that these questions also must be answered in the negative.

In its own peculiar way, this synthesis has committed all the errors to which we have called attention. By its interpretation of mind as the passive assimilation of fixed structure and its neglect of the concrete life-world, it has separated the objective universe of reason from the dynamic horizon of life and faith. By its doctrine of human reason as something divine, its view of metaphysics as a divine science, and its dogmatic restrictions on human freedom, it has confused philosophy with theology. By its reduction of faith to a set of opinions, or articles, about certain objects, and its attempt to combine these propositions with those of natural knowledge and to organize them logically into a great deductive system, it has confused theology with philosophy. To such a degree is this the case that through page after page in the *Summa Theologiae,* the careful reader is left in doubt as to whether he is reading deductions from the divine science of metaphysics or propositions of sacred theology, derived from revelation. By its theory of faith as a weaker reason bolstered up by authority in lieu of evidence and ultimately to be replaced by direct insight, it leads one to wonder whether this is not rather a subordination of faith to reason in the traditional Greek sense than a subordination of reason to faith in the Christian sense.

These errors have all been committed, and these questions must be asked. We need not conclude, however, that in intention at least this is not what it claims to be, a synthesis of Greek wisdom and Christian faith with the former subordinated to the latter as faith itself must demand. We must agree to this intention which shines through all the mistakes. We cannot agree, however, that this intention has been actually realized, even partially, in an adequate manner. Too many omissions and confusions blur the total picture. Authentic faith, as it is risked by living men in the contingent flux of history, is never clearly focused, and the free spirit of human reason is forced into the Procrustean bed of a special version of objective thought. What emerges is not so much the subordination of free philosophy to a concrete, living faith, as the subordination of one special philosophy to another triumphant version of the same, which is merged with Christian propositions.

This is not so much a synthesis as a confusion of pretentious philosophy with a rationalized version of faith. An adequate mode of synthesis still remains to be found. Nevertheless, Christian faith has been clearly distinguished from human philosophy, and we have been clearly warned against those confusions of the two which have plagued our Western history. In part, this has been due to philosophic criticism and analysis. But the gradual purification of faith, and the final secularizing of philosophy which has attended it, probably owe more to another kind of criticism coming from a very different source, to which we shall now turn.

4. *Apostolic Purification*

We have now examined three ways of attempting to reconcile the abstract perspective of reason with the concrete perspective of faith in the human *Lebenswelt,* the rationalistic way of Greek philosophy, the dialectical way of Augustine and Hegel, and the "religious" way of St. Thomas. Each of these has been thoroughly weighed and examined by persistent philosophical debate, which has shown them all to involve confusion, either an intermixture of the two, or a one-sided domination of the one by the other. But before we leave this subject, we must turn briefly to another more basic criticism coming from the *New Testament,* which has played an even more important role in revealing these repeated confusions throughout our history. This is the condemnation of rationalistic philosophy in the Epistles of St. Paul, especially I Cor 1:19–3:20, which has also been repeated in different times and circumstances by living traditions of Christian preaching.

St. Paul did not accept the Greek conception of the world (*kosmos*) as an all-inclusive order of nature, man, and gods, constituting a fixed, objective, cosmic frame. His conception was very different, following rather the Hebrew tradition in which he was reared. For him the world did not include God. It was not divine but created, and relative to man. The world means men in their entirety, together with all the things, events, and circumstances that move with men in their history. It is not a fixed, cosmological concept but is temporal rather than spatial. This world itself is historical, and is the broadest horizon accessible to our human understanding (*nous*). This understanding is not something divine in man. It is purely and inescapably human. It is, indeed, the inner man not as he brings himself as an object before the mind, but as he knows himself in the very act of living himself from the inside. Paul calls this knowing that proceeds with his being *suneidesis* or conscience (*con-scientia*). Since my being is ever directed ahead of myself toward projects which make demands, the conscience by which I know myself tells me of my future, and what it requires of me. It also leads me beyond myself to a transcendent source of authority on which my conscience is ultimately based. This conscience is not a special religious trait, but belongs universally to all men, including the heathen.[1]

It is only on the basis of this conception of human exist-

[1] Bultmann, *Theology of the New Testament,* I, 211 ff.

ence that we can understand the bitter condemnation of "philosophy and vain deceit" (Col. 2:8) and "the wisdom of this world" (I Cor. 1:20). This is not a condemnation of philosophic understanding in general as it has often been supposed to be, but of the pretentious claims of Greek rationalism, the only philosophy he knew. In this tradition, the Stoic sage claimed to know not merely a human world but a cosmic order in which the divinity itself was ever present, and moving in everlasting cycles. He claimed to be able to contemplate this divine system not by a merely human power but by a reason that was itself divine. Through this power he could bring not only external things but the human soul before the mind, analyze its different faculties, and calculate an order of acts that could lead it to happiness, and even to immortality.

Paul condemned these transcendental claims of reason as foolishness, and the continuous repetition and development of this criticism through centuries of Christian preaching has constantly reinforced those sporadic tendencies toward the humanizing of philosophy which were at last profoundly expressed in the thought of Kant. Since then, these tendencies have grown in strength. But as the tasks of objective observation and analysis were more and more taken over by the sciences, and as the concrete world of freedom, value, and risk was left to religion without any disciplined analysis, philosophy was deprived of its proper function, the revealing of human existence in the historical *Lebenswelt*. Abandoning the task that it alone could properly perform, it soon sank into a dependent and uncreative condition, content either to serve as the handmaid of religion in some form of fideism, or as the handmaid of science in some form of scientism. So we are now confronted by that radical separation of reason or rational science on the one hand, and faith on the other which is such a marked feature of the thought and the life of our time.

5. *The Separation of Reason and Faith*

If by faith we mean the ultimate concern for which we are ready to make real sacrifices in ordering our existence, and if by reason we mean the exact understanding of things around us and of our changing situation in history, it is clear that neither one can function adequately without the other. Reflection about an ultimate aim that loses touch with the actual problems confronting us ceases to reflect any real choice. It is the mere cultivation of an aim that is never really launched. Such fideism may be elaborately developed in terms of rigid scholastic formulations. But as it becomes increasingly remote from real life, it is also more open to the charges of arbitrariness and subjectivism which are often urged against faith itself, which is a serious misunderstanding. Without some living confirmation in terms of verifiable insight, the whole structure will be piously ignored until it is swept aside by cogent modes of analysis more in touch with the facts of life.

The basic neglect of philosophy which has been so characteristic of modern Protestantism has constantly exposed it to dangers of this sort. Thus American puritanism in the nineteenth century, oblivious to Biblical criticism and other developments of worldly thought, lapsed into an orthodox fideism which was more and more isolated from the living world and unable to defend itself against the advance of historical knowledge and philosophic criticism. Except where it was artificially protected, it fell before the attacks of a more cogently argued and empirically minded liberalism using methods of "objective analysis" which claimed to be uncommitted to any final direction. But such directionless analysis has difficulties of its own.

First of all, it is open to serious question whether the most "objective" analysis can avoid basic choices, though these can certainly be concealed, especially from the analyst himself. By his very projects, however, the analyst shows that he is basically concerned for this kind of truth, and for the pragmatic control over objects from which he is himself detached. This attitude may be defensible, as it certainly is in science. But it requires a defense against other possible alternatives. Is scientific truth the only form of truth? Are there other modes of being, for example, the free being of man, which cannot be understood in this way? The answer to such questions is not easy, and is not rendered easier by that absence of self-consciousness which is unfortunately so characteristic of scientism. Are there other aims more important than the manipulative mastery of external things? Are there other modes of understanding more sweeping and illuminating than objective calculation for power?

Its inability to work out a cogent answer to these questions and its attempt to escape from them, often leads to an instability in the objective mind which opens it to purely incidental and uncritical value judgments, and to forms of idolatry even worse than the urge to power. It is significant that totalitarianism dawned on a scene where liberalism was predominant, and that the chief opposition came from confessional groups which stood in the light of an ultimate choice. The most serious criticism of intellectualist analysis is perhaps its self-absence and lack of existential depth. Lost in objects of various kinds, and even an object to itself, the objectivist lives not so much in a world of his own as in a labyrinth of world-debris. Meanwhile the world moves on, and he is left behind, or passively swept into some blind and ephemeral commitment. Such is the unfortunate destiny of reason without faith, or ultimate fidelity.

It is a serious mistake to suppose that these factors, though always found together in the *Lebenswelt,* are joined in any natural harmony. Throughout our history they have been engaged in a constant conflict which has disintegrated countless lives and torn whole civilizations to pieces. But it is equally clear that each alone is imperfect and incomplete. One requires the other. The fideist knows where he wants to go but he has lost touch with the actual moving world. So he does not move, and goes nowhere. The liberal intellectualist, on the other hand, is at home in the moving world, or with some objective phase. He knows that he is going very fast, but knows not where he is going. On the one hand, direction without motion; on the other hand, motion without direction. In traditional terms faith should not be separated from reason. Neither a disoriented fideism nor an aimless intellectualism is tenable. Faith and reason somehow must belong together.

Nevertheless at present they exist apart in almost total separation.

6. *Christian Philosophy: Faith and Reason in Dialectical Tension*

I believe that we may learn something from this tortuous history of the relations between faith and reason which we have very broadly sketched. What has been called *reason* in our tradition is not in any sense divine. It is human, all too human, but if named in the right way without transcendental connotations, certainly not to be despised. It has no access to a fixed cosmic order of things in themselves, completely independent of man. It lives and functions in the moving world of history, where it has essential tasks to perform for each generation. These tasks are distinctive, and cannot be performed in any other way by any other discipline. Our review suggests that when it abandons these peculiar functions to render an ancillary service to science or religion, philosophy sinks into sterile verbalism and ceases to be. It is not meant to be the handmaid of anything.

When reduced to this state, it simply decays and becomes useless for any purpose. As its own history shows, it lives only in independence and freedom, and yet it is in some sense a discipline with access to a kind of verifiable truth. Can we perhaps call it the discipline of freedom? I believe that we can. But these assertions call forth certain questions.

If philosophy is not an objective science, to what kind of evidence does it then have access? What is its horizon? And how does it function therein? If it is really free, how then can it be a discipline? Are these ideas not wholly incompatible? If philosophy is neither to be confused with faith nor separated from it, as this review would seem to indicate, how then are the two related? Finally what can be meant by a Christian philosophy? How can this fail to be the sort of confusion against which our history so clearly and repeatedly warns? In the rest of this work we shall attempt to suggest a coherent answer to these questions. But here and now it may be well to suggest the form which this answer will take in a way that should be intelligible in the light of what has been said.

Scientific method abstracts from the subjective factors of experience in order to approach its objects from a detached point of view. Each special science singles out a special region to analyze and to explain within an objective frame. Philosophy is not a science. Its horizon is the historic world as a whole which envelops all human existence, including science. This world cannot be reduced to all the things in the world. It is neither an object nor any set of objects. Hence it cannot be analyzed and explained from a detached point of view, for it is impossible for any man or any attitude to get outside the world. It can only be understood and interpreted as it is lived from the inside. These are the peculiar functions of philosophy.

The first is a revealing function concerned with the direct evidence of lived experience which is neither exclusively subjective nor exclusively objective, but both together in one. In the light of this evidence and by the use of what are now called analytic or phenomenological methods, philosophy attempts to reveal the necessary structures which are always found in the *Lebenswelt,* such as lived space, lived time, and historicity. Here philosophy is concerned with the conditions of human freedom and its major possibilities rather than with the exercise of freedom itself. Immediate and constraining evidence can be found which calls forth intersubjective agreement. In exercising this revealing function, phenomenology can proceed with its own methods of verification as a discipline in the strictest sense of this word.

But the *Lebenswelt* is enveloped in mystery. In fact, it is only here that transcendence is actually glimpsed and encountered. Such experiences enable us to grasp the life-world as a whole, and call for a total interpretation. As our history clearly shows, it is religion that has always elicited that sweeping, synthetic speculation which is the second function of philosophy. Here the evidence is ambiguous, and open to divergent interpretations. It is at this point that philosophy has exercised the radical, noetic freedom which underlies its history in the West. In this history, we find different world-orders not only being constituted but also being brought into communication with one another.

These two functions, the understanding of freedom and its conditions, and the actual exercise of noetic freedom are distinct but mutually interdependent. Any decline in one is attended by a corresponding decline in the other. The second speculative function has been continuously performed throughout our Western history, but it has been seriously weakened and distorted by the gnostic neglect of the former since the time of Plato. This neglect of the *Lebenswelt,* first by Greek rationalism and later by objective science, is responsible for the marked separation of "reason" and "faith" which we have just noted as a basic feature of contemporary thought and life.

The most noteworthy philosophic achievement of our time is the rediscovery of the *Lebenswelt,* and those first disciplined explorations of it which have been carried out by recent phenomenology. This world of lived existence, the concrete world of man, contains the foundational data of the different sciences. It is from this world that they must begin, and from it, too, that they must derive their basic meanings and values. Freedom and transcendence are not objects. Hence they are necessarily reduced and deformed when placed within an objective frame. It is in the *Lebenswelt* that they are directly encountered. This world in a real sense lies between the objective perspective of reason and the subjective apprehensions of faith, and so, from its disciplined explorations, we may hope for a new approach to the problems of their reciprocal relations.

In performing its first function, revealing structures of the *Lebenswelt,* philosophy possesses a certain autonomy of its own. Within this field, as long as foundational concepts are left ambiguous, it can, like the special sciences, attain lasting clarifications and truths which are independent of ultimate interpretations. But such investigations are bound to be always imperfect and incomplete, for they rest on basic concepts like being, truth, value, and meaning which are partially indeterminate. Any attempt to complete the task (philosophy's second function) by a clarification of these terms must rest on faith in a guiding image of some sort that cannot be conclusively confirmed by any available evidence. This is proved by the history of philosophy. As is now well known, even science itself rests on assumptions of this kind which are not demonstrated, but remain ever ambiguous and subject to further change and clarification. So when a given assumption no longer seems fruitful in the light of the evidence at hand, we are always ready to modify or abandon it. In this sense, faith is dependent on understanding.

But our understanding cannot even get started without guidance of some kind. So the two are interdependent. And yet at the same time neither can be deduced from the other. Each is noetically independent. Our basic assumptions cannot be demonstrated by any available evidence. They must be accepted with genuine risk against other possible alternatives which are ever open. In this sense, faith is independent of "reason." But while it may guide us to look for certain things, it cannot dictate what these things will turn out to be. Here philosophy, like science, must follow the evidence alone. In this sense, it is independent of faith. Situations, as we know, constantly arise where the two conflict, where the evidence seems to discredit some basic assumption. Then a decision has to be made as to whether it should be dropped or modified in certain ways. In different senses one may be said to prevail, but neither can properly be said to be wholly ancillary to the other. This will lead only to blindness and confusion. But neither do the two fit into any reliable, pre-established harmony. We may only conclude that they are in a flexible, dialectical tension with each other. Like the two sides of the arch, each is dependent on the other, and yet at the same time independent, making its own contribution in its own way.

Christian philosophy is an enterprise of this kind. It is not a form of intellectualism, because it is aware of the human *Lebenswelt,* and does not believe that this concrete world can ever be squeezed into an objective, rational perspective. Like other modes of philosophy which have now learned something from our history, it is deeply concerned with the clarification and understanding of this *Lebenswelt.* But following the lead of the great thinkers of our past, it is unwilling to leave the task unfinished. Under the goad of transcendence, it is concerned with an ultimate interpretation, and accepts the risks involved, as indeed every man who is not content to merely drift with the current, must accept the risks in working out some view of himself and the world in which he lives. As other philosophers have taken their basic assumptions from images current in the culture of their times, the Christian philosopher openly accepts the guiding image of his faith in making ultimate clarifications where the evidence falls short.

Like the Augustinians, he realizes that without faith he will never gain understanding, but unlike them, he will carefully guard against any tyranny of the former over the latter. In dealing with evidence, he will follow it wherever it may lead, no matter how damaging this may be to what he thinks is the faith. Like Hegel, he will realize that faith without understanding lapses into sterile myth and fantasy. But unlike him, he will carefully guard against any unilateral assimilation of the former by the latter. The Christian philosopher will recognize that each has its own peculiar functions to perform in a genuine autonomy. Like Aquinas, he will see, nevertheless, that each requires the other. But unlike him, he will refuse to place them in a fixed hierarchical order or harmony, and to reduce either one to objective propositions and calculations. Faith and understanding cannot be placed and fixed in this way. They belong to the historical being of man, and as long as man lives, they will also live in dialectical tension with each other.

This is the meaning of that Christian philosophy which is now emerging as a disciplined endeavor for the first time in our history. In this volume, we shall try to introduce the reader to this discipline, in general (Chapters IV and V) and then more especially to Christian ethics and social philosophy (Chapters V, VI, and VII). But first we must face certain traditional objections which may be raised against the whole conception. To these we shall now turn in the following chapter.

Chapter Four

CHRISTIAN PHILOSOPHY AND
THE WORLD OF TODAY

In the first chapter we examined the transition from mythical to rational thought and life which marked the beginning of our Western history. We saw that in spite of its immobility and its incapacity to answer questions, myth enables us to grasp our lived existence in a concrete way which is closed to reason and science. This led us to raise the question as to whether we could find another alternative way of thought and life in our tradition which might offer us an escape from both the abstractions of science and the rigidity of myth. Can Christian philosophy offer us such an alternative? In the second chapter we examined Christian faith from this point of view, and showed how it differs from mythical life as well as from gnosticism. In our last chapter we turned our attention to the conflict between "reason" and "faith" which has plagued our Western history, and pointed out that if we look at this history carefully, it seems to suggest a conclusion.

Faith and reason cannot exist in separation. But neither should they be confused. Each of these extremes leads to serious difficulties. They must rather exist in a certain mutual tension in which each retains not only a certain autonomy but a certain dependence on the other. This also points to the need of attempting to formulate a Christian philosophy in living tension with the faith, a need which is now widely recognized by contemporary thinkers. In the second part of this work we shall try to explore this possibility. But before we embark on this quest, we must first examine some of the objections that have long been urged against any such attempt.

1. *Objections to the Idea of a Christian Philosophy*

There is no such thing as a Christian philosophy today. Moreover it is the concerted opinion of those historians who are best able to judge that there has never been a genuinely Christian philosophy in the strict sense of this phrase.[1] Finally, in recent debates on this subject, those who have held that such a philosophy will never be formulated have certainly had the best of the argument. The reasons they offer, largely derived from past conceptions of faith and reason, are indeed most cogent. Hence before embarking on a project of this kind, in which I shall attempt to reflect as a Christian on certain philosophic problems of our time, I think that it may be wise to consider these negative judgments and reasons, which arise both from the side of Christian faith as well as from the side of reason. First of all, let us listen to what is said on behalf of religion.

Protestant Objections

The most unqualified rejection of the notion of a Christian philosophy comes from Protestant sources, which from the time of the first reformers, have maintained a strong skepticism with respect to worldly philosophy. The fall of man has affected every human power, including human reason, which, as the history of philosophy shows, is incapable by itself of arriving at the truth, but brings forth only a confusion of inadequate and warring doctrines. This is true not only before but also after the Incarnation in the time of the Church Militant, during which, as history again

[1] Cf. Bréhier, *loc. cit.*

shows clearly, the disconcerting chaos persisted. Hence the complete autonomy of theology is cogently defended. So far as it can be understood, the Word of God must be understood by faith alone in its own terms without being subjected to the alien norms and structures of human philosophy. To those who are wise, in the worldly sense, the faith is foolish.

Any attempt to arrive at a synthesis of Christian faith with such worldly philosophy must result in a dilution and corruption of Revelation. Any continuous advance from rational thought to religion is out of the question. There is a radical break between the two. But a negative or skeptical approach is possible. By becoming sufficiently aware of the weaknesses and delusions of human thought, one may become disposed to Faith. The only Christian philosophy is the philosophy of no philosophy at all.

Catholic Objections

Catholics also reject the idea of a Christian philosophy, but for very different reasons. They point out that the Divine Revelation is directed to a limited human understanding in terms of which it must be understood, if understood at all. Theological discourse is intelligible and must, therefore, follow the rules of logic. Like all intelligible discourse, it must also use such terms as being, unity, man, space, time, and history, which belong to common experience and are open to natural modes of investigation. The clarification of such terms is not the peculiar function of theology, but belongs to an independent discipline (philosophy) which it must utilize for its own purposes. This discipline is developed by the unaided, natural faculties of man, which have a limited access to the truth even after the fall.

Since truth is one, these truths, when clearly grasped, must be harmonizable with Revelation. But there is no reason to consider this ancillary, or subalternate truth as specifically

Christian. It is presupposed by the different human sciences, and involved in the moral and political activities of man. To call it "Christian" is to confuse two distinct disciplines in a way which is extremely dangerous to both, encouraging each to advance beyond its necessary limits, and responsible for endless confusions. What theology needs is not a Christian philosophy, but simply sound philosophy. Such a sound, objective philosophy is not easy to achieve. But in so far as it is realized, it must harmonize with Revelation, for truth is one.

Objectivist Objections

Objective philosophers in the free universities are even more critical of the idea of a Christian philosophy, which would threaten the independence of their discipline. The very existence of science shows that the noetic powers of man have access to constraining, objective evidence, capable of convincing any trained observer. They contain within them the seeds of a rational certainty which far surpasses that of any uncritical belief bolstered up by organized authority. It is a crime against humanity to chain these powers, instead of allowing them to roam freely in following the truth wherever it may lead them. The history of science shows clearly that this freedom from external authority lies at the heart of this search for genuine, objective truth. The problems of philosophy are, no doubt, more complex than those of science. But there is reason to believe that with sufficient time and patience, similar results may be obtained in this field as well, granted a real freedom of thought which has never prevailed in the past.

Religions divide mankind into groups artificially separated from each other by subjective prejudices and passions disguised as revelations. Science, on the other hand—the work of human sense and reason—is international and universal. It enables men to co-operate under the guidance of confirmed, objective theory. We may reasonably hope, therefore, that, using methods of this kind, we may eventually arrive at an objective philosophy shedding some light on those basic problems to which passion and prejudice have succeeded so far only in giving us answers which are divided and partly blind. But to achieve this goal, philosophers must first be freed from any irrational commitments to religious theories deeply charged with feeling. Such commitments will only bias the mind of the observer, and thus continue to impede real progress. To argue for a Christian philosophy, therefore, is to abandon objectivity for the subjective. It is to turn the clock of scientific progress backward.

It is, indeed, amazing that two parties so strongly opposed on almost all other issues as Christians and anti-Christians in our present culture should agree with such unanimity on this unqualified rejection of anything like a Christian philosophy. These are certainly cogent arguments containing large elements of truth. They are strongly reinforced by other considerations coming from more neutral sources, which point to such a radical divergence between the experiences which lie at the root of religion and philosophy in the West that any attempt to synthesize them would seem to be impossible.

Anthropological Objections

These historians point to the basic shift from mythical, religious modes of reflections to rational thought which occurred in ancient Greece with the first origins of Western philosophy. This break is confirmed by anthropological studies which show how the static life-patterns of primitive society are governed by religious myths, and how human history became possible only through the destruction of these overarching structures of thought, and through their replacement by rational philosophy and science, which proceed by division and patient analysis. From this point of view, any attempt to formulate a really religious philosophy would be like an effort to end human history, and to revive the endless repetitions of archaic, mythical society.

Phenomenological Objections

Recent phenomenological studies have also emphasized the basic differences between the experience of the sacred, which lies at the root of religion, and the weighing of objective evidence, which lies at the root of what we now call *reason*. The former, as Schleiermacher saw, involves a feeling of dependence on something transcending our limited powers; the latter a sense of human independence and a desire for conquest. The former leads to the establishment of authority and attitudes of human abasement; the latter to the disestablishment of authority and attitudes of freedom. One leads to mythical modes of thought which are careless of incoherence and contradiction; the other to rational systems which are scrupulously coherent and logical. Religion involves a total response to the whole of existence which pervades every area of life. Thus Eliade, in his masterful study of the history of religions, shows how this response resists all limitation, and tends to absorb every phase of conduct until the whole of life becomes a liturgy.[2]

Reason, on the other hand, while it may attempt to guide all human endeavor, is only one mode of action among many. In connection with this, it is evident that religion includes subjective feelings and attitudes from which objective philosophy, by its very nature, must constantly try to abstract. Religious thought must be committed, while science and philosophy are objective and detached. These results are also confirmed by unbiased students of the Christian faith who point out that it cannot be understood as a theory *about* something, but rather as a total existential involvement of the whole person *in* something of ultimate concern.

[2] Eliade, *op. cit.*, pp. 366–367.

2. *The Answer of Christian Philosophy*

It would be silly to ignore this array of cogent argument which bars our path at the very beginning. It is also impossible to deny that there is much truth in these reasons, and that a negative conclusion of this kind, to which Christians, anti-Christians, and neutral observers all agree, must be taken seriously. There is no doubt that these arguments do apply to a conception of Christian philosophy which has been influential in our history and which is still alive today. But a further question must now be raised. Is this the only possible kind of Christian philosophy? Is there perhaps another kind to which these arguments do not apply? I believe that there is another kind which has not as yet been seriously thought through, and with which we are quite unfamiliar. I shall try now to suggest what this new mode of philosophy is by a critical examination of the arguments we have just presented with a view toward determining more exactly just what it is that they rule out. Then I shall turn to an exposition of the kind of Christian philosophy which they still leave open, the development of which is the subject of Part Two.

Reply to the Protestant Objections

So far as the Protestant case is concerned, we may agree with this cogent defense of the autonomy of faith which has its own ways of insight, not to be confused with the discursive methods of reason. God is not man and when He speaks, He speaks to us in His own way, not necessarily in accord with the norms and principles of human logic. This part of the Protestant argument is very sound. Any attempt to show how God must speak if He is to be understood by such and such a human faculty, or to interpret what He has said in terms of the fixed principles of any given philosophy must end in a humanistic dilution of the Word of God. Revelation must be understood in its own light, by faith alone, in its own way, which is not the way of any philosophy. Man may need philosophy. God certainly does not.

We must also accept the depressing judgment on the history of Western philosophy. As one who has spent a large part of my life in the study of this history, I may perhaps dwell for a moment on this point. Many attempts have been made to find a single order and meaning in this vast history as a whole. But success has been won only at the price of ignoring great parts of it *in toto*. It is not different doctrines that are in conflict here, but different human worlds. The world of Plato is not the world of Spinoza, and the world of Nietzsche is neither. It is not surprising that, since the time of Hegel, the study of the history of philosophy has suffered a decline. A skeptical conclusion is far too easy. This is what has happened to human minds which have tackled meaningless problems beyond their capacities, a weird confusion of fantastic dreams and arbitrary constructions. But men will not take seriously something which seems to lack all possibility of meaning. So philosophy itself, as an academic discipline, has also declined. Nevertheless it has persisted, for human life is impossible without some understanding of myself and the world in which I live. Philosophy is this understanding.

We may agree with this Protestant diagnosis, which, up to this point, is so close to the positivist analysis. But then we must ask, What should be done? That a necessary human activity should have fallen into corruption and confusion in the course of history is certainly in accord with Christian faith. This should be no surprise. What then is the Christian's duty? Should he wash his hands of this affair, and go about his proper business? What then is his business, or rather what is not? He himself is also in the world. The very language that he uses in expressing his faith is pervaded with philosophic meaning. This is where the Protestant case is very weak. This Christian philosophy of no philosophy— does it make sense? As Aristotle pointed out, skepticism is also a philosophy to which available evidence is relevant, and therefore no more justifiable before an examination of this evidence than any other. Can the honest Christian avoid such an examination? Can the Church avoid it? Is there any necessary mode of human action in the world which the Church can abandon without making a constant effort to rescue it from its lost condition, and to renew it into a sounder form? Is not this renewing of the intelligence a constant Biblical theme?

How then, in the light of the Gospel teaching, can the Church and the individual Christian avoid accepting a responsibility for the formulation and constant reformulation of a sound and genuinely Christian philosophy? I do not see how it can. Does this mean corrupting the Gospel with worldly philosophy? Of course not—no more than the Christian interest in improving medical service for the people must end by confusing the Gospel with medicine. The Gospel must be kept pure in its own light, and not mixed with human philosophy. But neither must it be hid under a bushel. The light is not corrupted by being allowed to shine. A Christian philosophy is not a system deduced from Christian principles. There are no Christian principles in this sense, and such a deduction is rightly feared as a corruption of both. Christian philosophy is not this at all. It is rather an attempt to bring the judgment of faith to bear on this activity of man, and to bring philosophy into such a condition that it can face this judgment, and be illumined by it. There is nothing in the Protestant argument which opposes such a conception of Christian philosophy. As a matter of fact, when properly understood, this argument favors it.

Reply to the Catholic Objections

The Protestants are afraid of corrupting the Gospel with false philosophy. They want to keep it so pure that they will not let it shine. Catholics, on the other hand, are afraid of interfering with the autonomy of philosophy as an independent discipline. They have an inadequate conception of the fallen state and present misery of man, especially as it affects the human intellect. Seeing that this intellect can still perform syllogisms, they diagnose it as essentially sound. But a syllogism only compounds error when false premises are fed into it, and they do not see the ways in which all the basic intellectual intuitions of man are now darkened and confused. This respect for the fallen intellect of man has led them to accept one human philosophy, to establish it as a tradition, and to reject the rest. They are thus able to make sense out of the history of philosophy by rejecting the last third, in which human subjectivity was finally focused. Their concern for the autonomy of philosophy has been so exclusive that they have failed to see the need of reviving and renewing it in the light of faith.[3]

Catholics are rightly afraid of authoritarian interference with the freedom of philosophic thought, though they still insist that it is subalternate to theology, which has a veto power over its doctrinal formulations. This fear is certainly justified in the light of the history of the Church. But Christian philosophy has nothing to fear from this sort of critique. This kind of thought, if it is ever formulated, will certainly be philosophy in the full freedom of its exercise from the most significant to the least significant of its doctrinal formulations. It will not be Christian in the sense that any of its assertions have been either deduced from or vetoed by revelation. It will be pure philosophy in conformity with its own kind of evidence available to all, and utterly different from

[3] Cf. Rom. 12:2.

theology. It will be Christian in the sense that, from the beginning and at moments of essential ambiguity, Christian faith will be present as a guiding spirit, and that at the end, it will be capable of illumination by the light of revelation. Such a philosophy will have nothing in it which is inaccessible to the revealing powers of man. Hence it will be straight philosophy with no admixture of theology, and not subject to this Catholic critique. But it will be a human philosophy guided by a Christian spirit, and always open to further illumination.

Reply to the Objectivist Philosophers

Turning now to the free philosophers, so sure that they are free, I must point first of all to the sad but evident fact that the great objective philosophy of which they have dreamed for so long in the West (2400 years) has not yet appeared on the scene. Instead of this universal system of thought, which would at last bind all men together intellectually and put an end to the chaos of history, something quite different has happened. Human history has happened. This history has gone on, and has produced an ever more bewildering and diverse array of opposed ways of thought, as though professional philosophers were really free. The dreamers of this great dream, and many still are dreaming it, have forgotten at least two important truths about human beings, each one of which deserves a brief comment at this point.

First of all, they have forgotten the personal existence which lies at the center of every human world. This personal center of action and meaning is not reducible to an object, nor to any set of objects. It is true that I may abstract from my own individuality and the world horizon in which I actually exist, in order to pay attention to certain objective facts about myself, or certain things which anyone, no matter who, may recognize. This is the reduced or impersonal "world" of objective philosophy and science, in which their technical discourse takes place. The dream of the objective mind is to make this "world" of objects all inclusive. The dreamers recognize, of course, that there is a quixotic factor not yet included in their great construction which they call "the subject." This subject is admittedly not known by objective methods, and does very strange and as yet unpredictable things. But given the solution of certain difficult problems, the time will come when this subject will be explained in objective terms. Then, the subject and his whole concrete world, at least in outline, will be absorbed within the real objective world of things as they really are.

This time, however, will never come. The objective method of science is always abstract, and leaves out many aspects and relations. It reveals not things as they are in their entirety, but perspectives on these things. Furthermore, the personal "subject," in his inner existence as he lives it, is not an object, and remains inaccessible to such objective observation. The world of everyday experience can never be ultimately explained and included within the "world" of objective things in the world. This is certainly not true, for the latter "world" is abstracted from the former, and, therefore, necessarily less rich and inclusive. It is only in the concrete life-world that we find things in their totality as they originally are. But this world is relative to an existing "subject" who organizes it and gives it meaning. Needless to say, it is this world, not the universe of science, which is the concern of all living literature, and most certainly of the Bible. It is also the horizon of the living language of ordinary discourse. When so-called moral issues arise between persons, for example, it is not two theories which are clashing, but two different worlds in conflict.

It is most important also to realize that philosophy is simply the disciplined study of world-formation, and that what we meet with in the history of philosophy is just what we meet with in alien persons, different ways of organizing the world, but worked out with more precision and care. This is true even of the great objective systems which dominate our intellectual history, for they are claiming to show that the concrete world of daily life can be organized in this way without residue. They are also concerned primarily with the *Lebenswelt*, though their exclusive claims are subject to serious question.

This leads us to a second truth about man which is forgotten by these objective dreamers. This is human historicity. These objective systems are closed. They claim to have access to a timeless truth in the light of which they can take account, in principle, of all that has happened and all that ever will happen. On the basis of such claims, schools are established which, apart from a few refinements, proceed to repeat this final truth over and over, as though history were at an end. This has occurred time after time in our Western history. One might even define a great objective thinker as one who makes the claim of ending our intellectual history. But the sad fact is, as we all now know, that history has gone on. Disciples have come with new meanings of their own, penetrating much deeper than any refinements, and the schools have passed away. New thinkers have come with systems of their own meeting new needs and new problems. So history has not ended. The human world itself is historical, and it is now clear that each generation, and, indeed, each new individual thrown into a new situation must develop new meanings, and work out his world in his own way. This is not the expression of an arbitrary wish or decision on the part of anyone. It is the expression of a hard truth about man. History cannot be stopped as long as man exists, for his very being is historical. Philosophy, therefore, by its very nature, cannot be terminated by man.

These facts are shocking to the objective mind, which does not like to dwell upon them. When pressed, it will defend itself by referring to historical relativism as the end of all truth and all responsible philosophy, meaning its own kind of philosophy and its own conception of timeless truth. We shall here make only a few comments on this situation from the standpoint of Christian philosophy which will interpret it in a very different way.

To the Christian philosopher it will come as no very great surprise that men have at last discovered that their being is historical. The Gospel itself is centered on certain historical events, and even the pagans and atheists among us measure their historic time by the Incarnation. Nor will he be surprised that the vast philosophic systems, constructed by men, which claim to know the timeless natures of all things and to put an end to history, have been revealed as a hollow pretense. God alone, not man, will bring history to its end, and it is only at this time that God, not man, will reveal the nature of all things in their true and final light. The effort of a single man, or group of men, to attain by themselves such knowledge and to answer the basic questions on behalf of all men until the end of time is an effort of man to be God that is doomed to failure. The Christian philosopher will take this lesson seriously, as part of that renewal of knowledge which is a constant theme of the Pauline Epistles.[4]

He will not, however, follow the positivist in concluding from this breakdown that the effort of philosophy is to be abandoned as meaningless. To renew the mind is not to abandon it. He will see in the act of understanding a necessary phase of his own existence, and a necessary phase of human being-in-the-world. Therefore he will not evade the task of seriously examining the basic questions underlying the process of interpretation, nor will he scorn the true results of such honest examination, even though he cannot hope that they will remain unchanged throughout future

[4] Cf. 2 Cor. 5:17; Rom. 6:6; Eph. 4:21.

history. He will be content if he can shed some light on his own problems and on the mysteries of his own world, and if he can help others existing in the world with him to shed more light on their own worlds in their own way.

The Christian philosopher will view a respect for the integrity of other human persons, and for their God-given capacity to give meaning to things as an important part of that "humbleness of mind" about which the Bible also speaks.[5] He will thus withstand the temptation of evading philosophy altogether. Neither will he embrace any form of the doctrine now known as historical relativism. He will be concerned with the working out of an open philosophy, doing justice, so far as possible, to the existence of his own contemporaries and to the knowledge of his time. If he proceeds in this way, he will have nothing to fear from the criticisms of objectivist philosophers or antiphilosophers.

Reply to the Anthropological Objections

Turning now to the anthropological criticism of Christian philosophy as a dangerous return to mythical thinking and the endless repetitions of primitive society, we must note, first of all, that in spite of the sensational triumphs of science and the coming of rational history, the myth has by no means disappeared. Far from it. We of the twentieth century have witnessed not a final clearing away of shadowy myths by the light of science, as the positivists led us to expect, but rather a great proliferation of new myths, especially in the political order, such as the Nazi myth of blood and soil, and the communist myth of the redemption-bringing proletariat. This suggests that the myth is not to be understood as primitive science but rather as another mode of understanding which grasps certain objects and does certain things which science cannot do. The widespread influence of myth in our time is such a striking phenomenon

[5] Cf. Col. 3:12.

that it has brought forth several penetrating studies which tend to confirm this impression.

Unlike science, the myth, as we have noted, is concerned with the life-world and its concrete manifestations. Since these manifestations can be understood only in their total world context, the myth is always governed by a global sense of wholeness. It is no accident that a philosopher, like Plato, wishing to convey a sense of the whole situation of man, tells us the myth of the Cave in Book Seven of his *Republic*. Science divides and analyzes. The myth is integrative and synthetic. Unlike science, which abstracts from all subjective feeling and value, the myth is pervaded by the concrete tang of existence. All the basic structures of human being, like temporality, death, choice, and all the values, pure and impure, are treated in the myth, not merely as objects but as they are lived and felt. Anxiety, for example, has no place in the attitude of the scientist himself, who treats it, therefore, only as an object placed before him. But in many myths the sense of this strange feeling is essentially conveyed.

Philosophy also is concerned with the life-world and with this world as a whole. As part of this total enterprise, it should be concerned not only with the abstract structure of objects but with subjective existence as well, though it must be granted that in the past it has neglected this part of its function. Of course there are striking differences, as the critics emphasize. Imagination is the tool of mythical thought which often uses this tool for the creation of total images which fall into incoherence, and have little respect for detailed evidence. Philosophy, on the other hand, while concerned with attaining a global view, must proceed step by step with disciplined attention to the evidence. Nevertheless it is fair to say that in our historical cultures, philosophy has been assigned the task that was performed by myth in primitive culture. How then is Christian philosophy to be understood in this context? Must it mean a return to mythical thinking and an abandonment of rational history? Or to ask the basic question: Is Christian Revelation the same as primitive myth?

The answer is *No.* As we have seen (Chapter II) there are many differences. But in this context a reference to one is sufficient. As the critics point out, the myths that govern primitive life take cognizance of time. But they seek to transcend it by lifting it up into a great time (a once upon a time) of heroic action which our human time, so far as it is worthy of attention, simply repeats over and over in an endless liturgy. Hence the world of primitive myth is radically unhistorical. It is not interested in any unique events as such, but only in events so far as they exemplify an archetypal action. The mythical mind is indifferent to the facts of history, or uses them only as a point of departure.

The Christian revelation, on the other hand, is primarily focused on just such unique, individual events. In fact these historical events lie at the heart of its message. If it could be shown, for example, by disciplined, historical research that no such person as Jesus of Nazareth ever existed, or that an important phase of his life, as told in the Gospels, never really occurred, this revelation would be deeply affected at its foundations. It is not a body of doctrine, nor a flight of the imagination, nor any combination of the two. To show that it was either of these would ruin it forever. This means that it is radically and basically historical. As a matter of fact, it was only through its influence that the Western mind was freed from the semimythical, cyclic views of Greek thought. There are also other ways in which it differs from modern myths. But its radical historicity separates it from any form of primitive myth.

Thus we may answer the anthropologists by referring to this sharp distinction. Christian philosophy is not a return to the repetitious structures of primitive life, but a way of thought determined by certain unique events in history and itself profoundly historical. Revelation is not the same as myth.

As over against the mythically inspired objective philosophers who are far more influential and typical of the West, there are a few exceptional figures whose thought, while seldom rounded, was nevertheless inspired by Revelation and who, therefore, can be called Christian thinkers. Revelation, while an organic whole, is too rich to be grasped in a single mood or image. Hence, in the first place, such Christian thought will be less systematic and broken into more diverse fields of interest. Second, such thought will be primarily concerned with actual history, and will distinguish very sharply between such history and myth. Third, this kind of Christian thought is moved by a transcendent message which is ever present, and to which it is constantly straining its existential effort and attention. Furthermore the message itself, though not mythical in form, is pervaded by existential understanding and passion. Hence thought of this kind will be less objective and more aware of the categories of personal existence. Three thinkers who exemplify these traits are Augustine, Pascal, and Kierkegaard.

The Christian philosophy we have in mind has nothing to fear from this anthropological criticism. Not only can we fairly say that it is not mythical; we can also say that it is far less mythical than other prevalent types of philosophy in the West. It is not only opposed to the repetitive structure of prehistorical societies, but in itself radically historical, and largely responsible for the full transition to a noncyclical conception of history. If we mean by philosophy a disciplined attempt to understand the concrete world in its full richness, both subjective and objective, with no intrusion of myth, this type of thought, if it were ever persistently pursued, would be philosophy par excellence. If it is essential to this mode of understanding to be free from all admixture of mythical interpretation, then this is an exceptionally pure mode of understanding, for it is bound to a radical distrust of myth by the historical nature of its foundations.

While the three thinkers mentioned do exemplify this mode of thought to some degree, they do so very imperfectly, for each of them had to devote much time and energy to polemics in the process of growing out of objectivist modes of thought. Thus Augustine had to struggle with Platonism, Pascal with the thought of Descartes, and Kierkegaard with the system of Hegel. And each of us is deeply affected and influenced by what he has to struggle against. It is, therefore, fair to say, as we have said, that Christian philosophy, as a clearly understood and persistent endeavor, has not yet come into being in the West.

Reply to the Phenomenological Objections

We must now consider finally the phenomenological objection to Christian philosophy, based upon the well-established differences between the attitudes of faith and those of reason. Religion involves a total human response which is subjectively committed, grounded on authority, and indifferent to human logic. Philosophy, on the other hand, involves a partial response to reason which is objective, subjectively unconcerned, independent of all authority, and bound to the rules of logic. In view of these radical differences, how can the two be brought together in any way which will avoid destructive reduction on the one hand, and eclectic confusion on the other? Such a philosophy must be in some sense Christian. But how is this possible without compromising the essential autonomy of philosophy? This question has really been involved in all the others, and it is time now for us to face it as such.

Let us begin with the situation of systematic theology which is best defined as a self-critical attempt to grasp the content of Revelation as an organic whole, allotting to each element its proper position in this whole without distortion or exaggeration. In this enterprise, faith, of course, is presupposed. Unless we have faith in the honesty and integrity of a human person who is revealing his mind to us, we cannot understand him. Similarly without faith in God, we cannot hope to gain any understanding of His revelation to us. But from this point on the two situations are radically diverse.

In the case of the human person, the normal feelings and categories of reason are usually sufficient. This is faith seeking philosophic understanding. But in the case of God, we are concerned with a being who transcends all our feelings and categories. Hence revelation can be understood only with reference to norms provided by itself. This is faith seeking its own autonomous mode of understanding, peculiar to itself. Nevertheless there is certainly one aspect of this work of faith where human philosophy comes into play. Any communication addressed to man must use language which can be understood by him in terms of his own being-in-the-world. Hence an initial philosophic understanding of the meaning of such terms as time, choice, freedom, anxiety, and man is required, though the further development of these terms is autonomous. Since the Biblical message is deeply concerned with the concrete *Lebenswelt,* any philosophy which is able to shed further human light on this world of our existence and its constant structures can offer real assistance to the faith. It is clear, however, that faith must play the guiding role in this quest for understanding. Hence the autonomy of theology is not jeopardized.

The situation of a Christian philosophy would seem to be quite different, however, for here something extraneous to philosophy (faith) would seem to play a guiding role. If in committing himself to some religion, the philosopher would maintain his own autonomy within his own province, it might be admissible. But if in committing himself to Christianity, he allows this commitment to influence his own procedures in constructing a Christian philosophy, how then can he avoid eclecticism and the loss of his own objective autonomy? This is the question which requires an answer.

The answer must begin with counter questions. Can even the most objective philosophy avoid all "subjective" factors? Can anyone start to philosophize with an absolutely empty mind? Can the human philosopher escape from an initial structure of meaning absorbed from his social milieu which determines the direction of his inquiry, and influences it at crucial moments of decision?

I believe that evidence brought forth in the age-long discussion of these questions must force anyone living today to a negative answer to all these questions. Even though it never appears in the objective panorama of a great system, there is always a mind that has thought, or now is thinking it. This mind was never empty, for wherever it was and whenever it started officially to philosophize, it belonged to a human person already existing in the world, and already possessing some mythical or intuitive grasp of his world. We have referred to the global intuition which lies at the root of the greatest of our Western philosophies. There is no doubt a creative factor at work in the formation of these mythical intuitions. But it would be hard to deny that they have also been affected by meanings and controversies current in the worlds of their creators. Sometimes this starting point of the point of view will be clearly marked, and it will be evident almost at once that the author is thinking as the member of a certain tradition, a nation, a class, or a school of thought in history.

Sometimes this structure of meaning and value, prior to the thought itself, is largely unconscious or semiconscious in the author. In this case, its distorting and limiting effects are more dangerous and more restrictive. Sometimes they are clearly focused and openly admitted. In this case, as we shall see, their effects are apt to be less dangerous. But to recognize objectively the limits of one's point of view does not necessarily imply a total escape from these limits. There is always a guiding image of meaning which underlies the whole inquiry, is never included within the system, and yet determines its general direction and scope.

We now have an answer to the phenomenological criticism which rests on the sharp separation of subjective faith from a purely objective philosophy. We reply that there is no such thing as a purely objective philosophy. Every system of thought rests on a global image of some sort that cannot be examined as an object from outside, and is in this sense "subjective." Every philosophy proceeds from the point of view of a guiding image of this kind.

We are not saying that such investigations are, therefore, worthless and incapable of achieving any truth. This would, of course, be equivalent to absolute skepticism, for all human inquiries are perspectival and therefore limited in this way. But because I see something from a certain perspective does not mean that I do not see it. I see orders of meaning and value that really exist, because I exist. But there are also other orders that I do not see, and if I yield to the temptation of supposing that this is *the* world, I am in danger of falling into grave distortions and errors. The reason I am so susceptible to this temptation is that I see the things that lie within the perspective so much more clearly than the perspective itself and its originating structures. In order to see this, I would, of course, have to get out of my perspective, and enter another with different limits. But while I cannot see this perspective from the outside, I can become aware of my own originating meanings from the inside as I express them. If some limiting structure of meaning is necessary, as I believe it is, and if the purpose of philosophy is to use our human faculties in achieving a global insight into the *Lebenswelt,* which to some degree escapes from these limitations, then it is possible to discuss what sort of originating point is best adapted to this end.

What sort of guiding image is apt to elicit from the disciplined thinker an understanding of the world that is least affected by human limitations? We shall now conclude with a consideration of this crucial question.

3. Faith as a Guiding Image for the Christian Philosopher

Of course the standard procedure of most philosophers in the past has been simply to forget about this problem, and to plunge right into the business of philosophizing, the assumption being that they were starting with an empty mind, and no presuppositions. Then they have proceeded to work out the timeless truth about God, the world, and man with little self-consciousness, as if all this came from no point of view at all. We are far from saying that no truth was discovered by such nonreflective procedures. But we now know that they did proceed from mythical images of meaning, absorbed and reconstructed from their own time and milieu. Very often these guiding images were sufficiently sound and fertile to enable them to see a great many things, and to arrive at structures of meaning still living in our current speech. We are far from belittling this achievement. But they suffered from a most unfortunate blindness, which led them to suppose that they were starting with no initial meanings, and arriving at a closed and timeless truth.

This blindness was due to a lack of existential self-consciousness which is hard to defend today, for we are aware that history was not ended as it should have been. In completing their systems, they were not putting the finishing touches to human intellectual truth. We are still searching, and will be searching until the last man dies. This is why we can no longer follow the self-oblivious method, as we may call it. Some among us, too attached to the past, seem to think that this must mean the end of all philosophy which cannot be reconciled with the limitations of a historical point of view. No competent thinker can start philosophizing today in a serious sense without reflecting on the meaning of his project. What are the global meanings that are guiding his endeavor? What is his point of departure, and where in general does he wish to go? Such questions must be raised. How can they be answered? What are the main alternatives, and what criteria are relevant to a choice?

I believe that the purpose of philosophy is to gain an understanding of the *Lebenswelt* which avoids the errors of partiality, inaccuracy, and superficiality. This implies three criteria in terms of which any point of departure may be judged. The first is wholeness. What is needed is a global view which leaves out no essential structure of this concrete world. In order to achieve this, the philosopher must make an effort to get outside of himself, and even to arrive at a standpoint which is outside the world. Of course this may be impossible. He may be deluding himself. Nevertheless the effort to gain such a transcendental standpoint is clearly discernible in the history of Western philosophy. Thus Plato, for example, seeks what has been called a *holoscopic* view of the world in the light of the good which is beyond our human existence, and even beyond all being.[6]

The second criterion is an analytic clarity which is in a sense opposed to the first. We may gain a total view that is nevertheless confused with respect to important parts, and which is, therefore, evidently inadequate. In addition to wholeness, we need also to achieve an insight into essential parts. This motive is clearly manifested in the so-called analytic philosophy of our time. But long before this, it was expressed in the *meroscopic* thought of Aristotle, who distrusted loose, synthetic views, and devoted his attention to

[6] *Republic* 509.

a careful scrutiny of essential parts, one by one, in order to attain a detailed accuracy. His position may be symbolized by that of a seeing eye. Such a thinker must get outside of each object that he looks at. He can see other persons in this way, and can even regard himself in a mirror, and thus gain a certain objective self-consciousness. But no eye can see its own seeing. This objective awareness of self is restricted to external traits and is, therefore, lacking in existential depth, which brings us to the third criterion.

It was not until modern times that this sort of critical self-consciousness became a problem for professional philosophy. But since there is no thought without a human thinker, even the most objective systems contain moments of self-criticism, and it is possible to use this as a criterion in judging the works of different philosophers. In ancient times, the self was generally treated objectively as a soul, and this element was never highly developed. It is fair to say, however, that it is less absent from the thought of Plato than from that of Aristotle. In the Middle Ages, Augustine and the Augustinian tradition have more existential depth than Aquinas and the Thomistic tradition, and in the nineteenth century Kierkegaard is more self-conscious than Hegel.

Holoscopic thinkers, of course, make objective observations. But as they make them, they may be aware of their own acts, and may be deeply concerned with the meaning of what they discover for their own existence. This is what I mean by existential depth. The existential thought of our time has been named with reference to this dimension. Such thought possesses existential depth but is so far lacking in scope. It is highly self-conscious but narrow in range, and open to the charge that it expresses a radical anthropocentrism. Classical thought, on the other hand, possesses scope and accuracy but is lacking in existential depth. What sort of guiding image might be most likely to meet all of these criteria and to develop a mode of thought that is neither partial, inaccurate, nor superficial?

I think that this question should be answered as follows. In order to achieve scope, the starting point should be as remote from our world as possible, for it is only from such a transcendent point of view that a global insight can be attained. Nevertheless in order to achieve accuracy, the guiding image must be also close to us in the world. Finally in order to achieve depth, it must have germinal feelings for the significance of personal existence. As we have suggested, the different intellectual traditions to which we now have access roughly fall into two groups. On the one hand, there are the objective schools which offer a high degree of scope and objective accuracy but are lacking in depth. Their guiding images transcend the world, or at least many parts of the world, but are not close enough to our subjective being to achieve existential penetration. As we can say in a summary manner, they offer a high degree of transcendence but insufficient immanence.

On the other hand, there are the "subjective" schools which meet the criterion of existential depth but fail to meet those of scope and objective precision. They offer a high degree of immanence but insufficient transcendence. Where can we find a guiding image endowed with a capacity for both transcendence and immanence, a structure of meaning and feeling, therefore, which is capable of being discursively developed into a philosophy which is neither partial, nor inaccurate, nor superficial?

I suggest that there is an image of this sort still living in our culture. This is the body of meaning and feeling which constitutes the Christian Revelation. That it is not an incoherent jumble of disparate fragments is shown by the existence of a systematic theology which to some degree has succeeded in grasping it as an organic whole. Of course it is certainly not a philosophy, though it has a unique structure of its own, which has a meaning for philosophy. But this has led to serious confusions in the past, and must always lead to confusion. We are suggesting that it might be accepted as a guiding image, an initial starting point for a philosophy, and, as we have seen, no human philosophy can come into being without such a starting point. Indeed, in the past, many great and influential systems have been developed from images of a wholly mythical character with nothing to show that they were anything more than chaotic fancies. Of course there is little evidence to indicate that such an image can serve as the guide to a sound and coherent rational thought, for there is as yet no such Christian philosophy. As we have seen, any persistent attempt to do this has been judged, and is still judged by competent experts, to be doomed to failure. Nevertheless in the light of the criteria we have been considering, there are reasons for believing that such an attempt might be worthy of a trial.

In order to attain a global perspective, the human philosopher must have access to a guiding image which establishes him beyond the world. That philosophers have found images of this sort is readily attested by a reference to the history of philosophy. We have already mentioned the mythical origins of Plato's philosophy, and how they encouraged him in his endeavors to see everything in the light of the transcendent idea of the good. St. Augustine believed that God was a living presence in his mind, constantly communicating to him a sense of His eternal and timeless truths. This mythical picture underlies the most cogent arguments of his philosophy. Kant's pietistic image of a God of stern justice, the Primal Being, stirring our reason to unceasing efforts of synthesis but inaccessible to them as their limiting idea, enabled him to achieve a global view of that human aspiration to which science and reason belong as essential parts. Hegel speaks of his logic as the structure of eternal ideas in the mind of God before the creation. This mythical picture lies at the root of his great system of philosophy.

These are at best only fragments torn from the full context of Christian Revelation. If such fragments as these have enabled philosophers to gain some freedom from the chains that bind them to an inner-worldly perspective and to see the world as a whole, why should not the unexpurgated Christian image function even more effectively? Does it not claim to emanate from the transcendent God Himself? Does it not lead faith to what is wholly other than itself? Would it not lead any listening philosopher to a point of view as far beyond himself as this is possible for man? Could it fail to encourage him to use every facility at his command to achieve a view of himself and the world that is global and impartial?

How about the factor of immanence? Here we must remember that the Incarnation is the central dogma of Christian faith. It is not that the transcendent God approached very close to man and the human world. He broke into this world, taking the very flesh of man upon Him, working with earthly matter, sailing on earthly waters, gazing at the starry heavens, feeding on animal flesh, acting and suffering in the events of worldly history. The story of this earthly life is not interpreted for us in terms of human philosophy, for this we can work out for ourselves. It is not spelled out in terms of science, for this we can do alone. But how could it fail to stir those who have been moved by this image to that profound interest in physical events which underlies our human science? Indeed it is no accident, as scientists themselves have pointed out, that under this impact, the human sciences received their major impulse. This is immanence par excellence. How then could a human philosopher, moved by this image, fail to be concerned with the individual things of this world of life, and the basic structures underlying them? How could a faith-image of this sort fail in the long run to elicit accuracy as well as scope?

But it was human flesh that God took upon Himself. It is man with whom this message is primarily concerned, not merely with man as he appears outside to others but with his inner heart and lived existence as well. "Thou blind Pharisee! cleanse first that which is within the cup and platter, that the outside of them may be clean also" (Mat. 23:26). We are told that this "inner" existence, from which the observable events of human history take their origin, is of interest to God, and possesses an eternal significance. Indeed, it is hard to see how the Incarnation can be otherwise interpreted. But if God is concerned with the heart of man —the feelings and choices that are his existence, how then can a philosopher, who accepts this image as his starting point, fail to be concerned with human existence, not merely the existence of others, but his own thought, his own feelings and choices, his own existence as well? Unless he betrays the spirit that is guiding him, can he fail in his reflections to become acutely self-conscious? Will he not be led to strain all his powers to the last degree in attempting to achieve depth as well as accuracy and scope?

This then is our answer to the criticism urged by phenomenologists that a Christian philosophy must involve a confusion of two attitudes, the religious and the philosophical, which are strictly different, and must end in a relaxation of standards that is particularly dangerous to the autonomy of philosophy. We have pointed out that no philosophy is perfectly autonomous in the sense that it starts with an empty mind. Every philosophy begins with a value image already present in the mind which determines its point of view, and to which the view itself is often blind. If this guiding image is never clearly focused, as in most rationalistic systems, it takes the place of evidence. Every move is determined a priori by this image rather than by the evidence, and the whole philosophy becomes a gigantic rationalization.

This has often happened to Christian thought in the past. Such philosophy is nothing but a sterile rationalization of a theology cut up into separate propositions, and thus deprived of its organic unity. When, however, the autonomy of faith, and the unique, organic unity of theology are recognized, this need not happen. Such a guiding image can be clearly focused without admixture and confusion. While offering philosophy a firm and definite point of departure, such a clear-cut image is flexible enough to leave philosophy free to follow its own norms in examining the evidence as it comes, without external interference, or, in other words, to give guidance in moments of critical ambiguity rather than a constant, rigid control.

While such a flexible partnership has been achieved only very rarely and intermittently in the past, we can see nevertheless, in two such thinkers as Pascal and Kierkegaard, how such a co-operative separation of theology from philosophy has brought forth purely philosophical insights of extraordinary significance. We have tried to discover the reasons for this in our discussion. As against other mythical structures, traditionally employed by philosophers, the Christian image is peculiarly rich in uniting into an organic whole factors of transcendence, immanence, and existential concern. It is not surprising, therefore, that in the exceptional cases where it has been utilized, this image, far from jeopardizing the autonomy of philosophy, has, as a matter of fact, helped it to follow its own peculiar way. This is not to say that such fruitful co-operation between independent disciplines can be realized without agonizing tensions which are manifested by the authors cited. But these tensions can be far more fertile, and far less confusing than the rigid imposition of a hierarchical order.

We have now completed the introductory portion of this study (Part One). In Chapters I and II we considered the differences between Christian thought and myth, as well as those between Christian thought and rationalism. Then in Chapter III we studied the age-long controversy of faith versus reason and criticized certain influential "solutions" of this issue. As a result of this study, we concluded that no such "solution" can end the living tension between the two, and that this tension calls for a Christian philosophy which is, on the one hand, independent in following evidence of its own, wherever it may lead, and yet, on the other hand, dependent on faith for certain decisions where the evidence is ambiguous. In this chapter (IV) we have considered some basic objections against the whole project. Now, having prepared the way, we are ready in Part Two to embark on the project itself and to deal directly with certain problems of Christian philosophy.

Part Two

CHRISTIAN ETHICS AND
SOCIAL PHILOSOPHY

Chapter Five

THE METHOD AND CONTENT OF
CHRISTIAN PHILOSOPHY

In this part we shall be concerned not with antecedent
problems but with questions arising in the field of Christian
philosophy itself. In this chapter we shall examine its
general method and content, and how it might be taught.
In Chapter VI we shall be concerned with Christian ethics
and how it differs from that ethics of self-realization which
has dominated rationalistic moral thought in the West.
After this, in Chapter VII we shall turn our attention to
social structure, to the strange and seemingly unbridgeable
gulf that yawns between individual and social action, and
to their respective norms.

Finally in Chapter VIII we shall present certain criticisms
of traditional theories in the field of social philosophy.
Then in the light of recent phenomenological research, we
will give a different account of the relation of the individual
to the group, and will suggest a way of bridging the chasm.
With this exploration of Christian ethics and social philosophy we shall end our present study.

In the preceding chapter, we considered certain objections
that have been raised against the idea of a Christian philosophy from Catholic, Protestant, and secular sources. These
objections hold against many Christian philosophical syntheses that have been constructed in the past. As we have
seen, such syntheses either restrict the autonomy of faith and

are not truly Christian, or restrict the autonomy of reason and are not truly philosophical, or constitute a mixture which is neither truly Christian nor truly philosophical. A critical study of the course of Western thought would seem to justify the judgment of the great French historian, Bréhier, that no genuine Christian philosophy has ever been formulated in the West and that the term is actually non-designating. This is not enough to prove, however, that it is not a real possibility, and we offered reasons indicating that the formulation of an autonomous philosophy based on secular evidence available to all but inspired by Christian faith as a guiding image was still possible. We saw, indeed, that this argument has further implications. Every philosophy requires a guiding image of some kind, and in comparing different types of image, it became clear that Christian faith has certain distinct advantages with respect to philosophic scope, accuracy, and existential depth.

This argument, I believe, is sound. But so far we have been concerned only with an unrealized possibility, and the argument has, therefore, been very abstract and remote. The case for a living concern with Christian philosophy would be enormously strengthened if we could find a way of challenging Bréhier's negative judgment, and if we could point to some concrete example of an important thinker, preferably in a modern context, whose secular thought was actually guided by a Christian image. Is there any modern philosopher who pursued his studies in a genuinely autonomous way, and who was led by Christian faith to sound and fruitful secular insights? Is any such example to be found?

There is such an example. I wish to begin by considering this example, and commenting on his significance for the general project of formulating a Christian philosophy which is, I believe, one of the great living possibilities of our time. After this I shall consider, in the second place, the descriptive method and content of such a philosophy, and third, a basic issue with which this method has confronted us. Fourth, I shall turn to the speculative and metaphysical aspects of Christian philosophy, and finally, fifth, to the way in which this subject might be advanced and taught in a Christian college or seminary.

1. Faith as a Guiding Image for the Thought of Kierkegaard

As is well known, Sören Kierkegaard, the Danish thinker, was brought up in a Christian home and, through his aging father, was given a profound sense of the meaning of religion. He was led to read deeply in Biblical literature and to embark on a course of training for the ministry. At the same time, he was steeped in the classics of Greek philosophy, and wrote his master's thesis on the irony of Socrates. He knew medieval theology well, and a set of St. Augustine's works is known to have been in his library. He was also deeply concerned with the thought of his own time, and in particular with the reigning philosophy of Hegel. He was extremely sensitive to the style and atmosphere of what he read, and was able to think for himself. One thing especially struck him in the Biblical writings which set them apart from all the philosophy with which he was then familiar. These writings were not concerned with formulating theories about things and persons from a detached, objective point of view. Nevertheless it seemed to him that they were pervaded by a very deep and accurate understanding of human life, not as viewed from the outside, but as existing from within. This kind of understanding he found nowhere in classical or modern philosophy, except in a few striking figures, especially in Socrates, and probably in Augustine.

Contemporary thought was completely dominated by a vast conceptual system including nature, God, and all the periods of human history, with a place, as he put it once, for everything except the existence of finite, fragile human individuals as they live it from the inside, perhaps in contentment, or in misery, in anxiety, despair, or possibly in faith and love. He found no understanding of these things in the philosophical literature of his time, where they were dismissed as purely psychological or "subjective." And yet it seemed to him that these matters affected the whole way of life of a man and the very world in which he lived to its outermost boundaries. In the Bible, he found that they were etched out in a strange and penetrating light which enabled him to understand his own world better, and the worlds of other men. This was surprising to him, as he was a mere youth with only limited experience, and by no means certain of his faith. What then should he do?

The obvious thing would be to continue his training as a minister in the National Church, then to bring out these long neglected meanings as meanings of the faith, and to publish them in works of Biblical exegesis and theology. This way he did not follow. Faith, he saw, had also been placed in a neat, objective compartment, called *the subjective,* and thus isolated from the rest of life. Christianity was no longer thought of as a way of existing with a world of its own. It had been so reduced to speculative objectivity that it now stood for little more than a fleeting assent to certain propositions which everyone in Denmark took for granted, since they made little difference in any case. There was little hope here of leading people toward serious, self-conscious reflection on themselves, little hope, indeed, anywhere. But the profound influence of Hegelian thought showed that his contemporaries still had a certain respect for the revealing power of secular reason. So he chose the very opposite course.

Instead of becoming a minister, he abandoned his career in the Church to devote himself to secular experience, and the writing of those inimitable, early works, signing them with pseudonyms to keep them free from any religious suggestion associated with his name, in which, with no overt reference to religion at all, he tried with all the force of his gifted imagination and his literary genius to express some of the basic truths of New Testament anthropology in secular terms sufficiently penetrating and sufficiently vivid to lead men around him to pay attention and really to think about themselves.

In classical thought, the world (*kosmos*) is viewed as a hierarchy of beings whose structure is already fixed apart from human choice. Man is fitted into this closed system and occupies an intermediate position in the hierarchy. He has nothing to do with determining the meaning of this world—unless he misunderstands it. His proper function is to let its real, cosmic meaning float into his empty mind from the outside, and then to adjust himself to it as it already is. The general pattern of the good life he is to pursue has been inscribed forever on his nature. His freedom has no effect on this *end*. It is restricted to a choice of means within his reach.

In the New Testament, the term *kosmos* is employed in a very different way. Take, for instance, the saying in the Gospel of John: "He was in the world—and the world knew Him not" (John 1:10). Many other examples of this sort could be quoted from the Johannine literature and the Pauline Epistles. The term *world* in these passages does not refer to a fixed, objective cosmos, existing in complete independence of man. It refers rather to man and his world *together*, to man as existing in a certain condition in a world that is relative to him. In his early work *Either/Or* and his later work *Stages on the Way of Life,* Kierkegaard tried to work out this man-world conception, showing in a purely phenomenological manner, without any special appeal to faith, how, in fact, the basic choice of a way of life affects not only the thought of the human individual, the way he understands himself, but his feelings, his action, the objects of his attention, and the whole structure of his world.

It is, of course, not necessary to point out that the human *Lebenswelt* has now become a dominant theme, not only of theological reflection but of secular philosophy in Europe. Thus in his last published work, the *Krisis der Europäischen Wissenschaften,* Husserl is basically concerned with this *Lebenswelt,* and says that it is subjective and relative to man. That man exists necessarily in a world, and that he exerts at least some control over its *meaning* is now accepted as a fact, accessible to anyone who will take the trouble to look at the evidence, by such wholly non-Christian phenomenologists as Heidegger and Jaspers, and even by the atheist Sartre. I simply bring this up as an example of fruitful results that have been achieved in philosophy by following through, in its own way, certain hints in the Biblical literature. There are, of course, many more that I can only mention.

For example, we have noted how the tradition tends to restrict human freedom by enclosing it within the structure of a world that is essentially finished.

In the Bible, however, human freedom is indirectly underlined and expanded. The whole Biblical *kerygma* puts the human individual and his existence in question. It confronts him with a basic choice on which his whole being and world will depend. The Biblical writings are pervaded by a poignant sense of a human time that cannot be reduced to a bare succession of nows. It is rather a time whose phases are joined together. The individual is held in the grip of a sinful past that binds him here and now; he exists in a present moment still open to final choices; he faces an eschatological future that will reach an end. The Bible itself reveals certain events not only in human history but central to human history. Even pagans now measure historic time by these events. The Bible does not present us with any theory *about* history. To those with faith it reveals something of its meaning and end. According to it, this is the ultimate perspective, and all human theories and philosophies, no matter how sweeping and vast, are themselves included within this historical perspective.

There is not time here to review in detail the way in which Kierkegaard took up the Biblical themes of conscience and choice, human death, human time, and history, and developed them, especially in his *Concluding Unscientific Postscript,* but also in other philosophical works, with no appeal to faith, but with extraordinary acuteness and observing power. Of course Kierkegaard failed completely in his attempt to awaken his contemporaries, by philosophical reflection, to the revealing power embodied in their own existence, which he called the subjectivity of truth. He was regarded as an eccentric crank, the reign of Hegelian habits of thought continued until its collapse at the turn of the century, and Kierkegaard's works gathered dust on the shelves of a few comprehensive libraries in the Western world. But one cannot say that he simply failed.

In the 1920's his works were rediscovered, and reputable thinkers began to see their power and their revolutionary implications. With the reinforcement of another empirical stream of thought (phenomenology), going back to the medieval concept of intentionality, and running through Brentano and Husserl, the thought of Kierkegaard underwent an extraordinarily rich and fertile development in which purely secular thinkers as well as Protestants and Catholics have all shared. His works have been translated into almost every important living language including Chinese, Japanese, and Korean, and it is now fair to say that his ideas are almost as widely known and as influential in the world as those of his great opponent Hegel, still the most potent of world philosophers. It is still too early to attempt any judgment on this movement, for it is only just beginning, and its final direction is unclear. It is already clear, however, that it has radically altered the course of philosophical and theological thought in the West.

I hope it is clear that I am not defending the thought of Kierkegaard as the final achievement of a Christian philosophy. It is seriously defective on many points, both theological and philosophical. His interpretation of the sacraments and of the Church as the body of Christ is deficient. His social philosophy is weak, and his justifiable attack on the divinized reason of the Western tradition, which received its last expression in Hegel, sometimes led him to excessive extremes. I am not suggesting that we all become Kierkegaardians. I am pointing to him as an illuminating example of autonomous, philosophic thought inspired by the Christian faith.

In considering this question, I have suggested that we might consider the organic content of the Faith not as a set of propositions from which, with the aid of rational first principles, philosophic conclusions can be deduced, but rather as a guiding image, indirectly indicating ideas, atmospheres, and modes of approach that can then be worked out in a purely secular way, and tested by secular evidence available to all, without jeopardizing the autonomy of the field in question. This sounds possible. But it is very formal and abstract. Has anyone ever done this? Where is an illustration to be found? The name of Kierkegaard is certainly relevant in this connection. Here is a man whose whole thought was inspired by the Biblical literature; his secular writings, and that means most of his works, are simply the secular development of certain Biblical themes.

And yet he goes out of his way, to the most tortuous extremes of his maieutic method and his use of pseudonyms, to avoid any confusion of human understanding with faith. In this secular field, he avoids anything remotely resembling an appeal to dogma or authority of any kind. His aim, as he put it, is to use a maieutic method to betray his reader, by an intensification of his own self-consciousness, into a pathway that leads to Faith. This is a perfect example of what I mean by a Christian philosophy, something that is both genuinely Christian, and at the same time genuine and undiluted philosophy. His insight is justified by rational evidence alone, but formed under the guidance of faith.

2. *The Human* Lebenswelt

The Bible does not speak the abstract, technical language of any science or objective philosophy. It speaks the living, or as we now say, the ordinary language of the human *Lebenswelt* with its full array of richness, feeling, tone, and ambiguity. To the scientist, this concrete world, in which we actually live and exist, is a chaotic confusion from which he must abstract to exercise his special methods of investigation. To the objective philosopher, like Plato, it is a Cave of shadows from which we must escape to gain overarching vision and clarity. Nevertheless this is the concrete world in which we are born, in which even the scientist struggles for his human purposes, and in which we die. This is the human world which we feel around us, understand to some degree, and express in the words and phrases of our mother tongue. As we have seen, this is the world of the Bible which, under its guidance, Kierkegaard began to explore.

It is true that the order of this world is not like the abstract laws and structures of science. Nevertheless it has an existential order of its own that is neither exclusively objective, nor exclusively subjective, but both together in one. In his penetrating descriptions of human time, anxiety, despair, choice, and history, Kierkegaard inaugurated the disciplined exploration of this life-world, and his initial investigations, as we all know, have now been crowned with many fruits. To maintain and to advance this investigation of the *Lebenswelt* is a major task of Christian philosophy. We shall have no time for an exhaustive account of the many things which have been discovered since the time of Kierkegaard. But I may be able to call the reader's attention to certain features of the *Lebenswelt* which will certainly be recognized as themes of major importance in any genuinely Christian philosophy devoting its primary attention to human existence as it is lived in the concrete world of everyday.

No living organism can be adequately understood without an understanding of its life-field. The inner cycles of its bodily life define an objective territory with certain traits which are necessary to existence. This existence depends on the field which conditions it. But the field depends on the type of organism which carves it out and gives it vital meaning. This is a strange *sui generis* relationship in which each factor is dialectically conditioned by the other, and which cannot be understood in terms of cause and effect. To live is to radiate. Hence each individual plant and animal not only has, but must have, a vital field into which its existence is projected.

The human being is no exception to this rule. He also has his vital field, or habitat, where he knows his way, and where his presence is radiated. He has the house and the family where he is at home; the carpenter has his shop where he works, the scholar his library where he studies, and the class room where he argues and teaches, the farmer his field and barns where he lives on the land. The individual becomes attached to his vital field and cannot be separated from it without becoming displaced and disoriented, as the city man in the country, or the peasant who gropes for his way in the city. Without roots in a vital field of this kind the normal person can do nothing. Blown this way and that by the varying winds of social change, he lives no life of his own. Floating about on the surface of things, his existence becomes deformed and contracted. He may be willing to lose himself in the anonymity of the masses and thus win a shiftless and shifting peace. But if he clings to his own existence, he will be forced to a bitter struggle that may end in sickness and death.

There are many structures peculiar to the *Lebenswelt*. The most important of these are self-conscious activity, global meaning, and transcendence, about which I shall now say a few words.

As Husserl pointed out, the *Lebenswelt* is relative to the human person who is always its center. This center is constituted by acts which manifest themselves in their very act by a knowledge which is immediate and indubitable. It is only through such knowledge in the *Lebenswelt* that I become directly aware of my own existence, and of alien existence that helps or threatens me. I express such self-awareness when I seriously use such phrases as *I mean, I think,* or *I promise.* This personal existence is never an object, and cannot be understood by any objective approach. The word *I* does not refer to anything else, nor does it refer to itself as an object, for this *I* is not an object. It is the expression of an active awareness, a source of purposes and intentions that is the center of the *Lebenswelt*.

In the second place, the *Lebenswelt* is pervaded by global meanings which, unlike facts, are to some degree subject to individual choice and control. Facts belong to no one. They are simply so. I do not speak of *my* facts, or *your* facts, Anglo-Saxon facts, or Hindu facts. But I may very well be asked to explain *my* meanings, and it is proper to speak of Western and Hindu meanings. The basic philosophic meanings which guide our existence (like being, freedom, man, and meaning itself) have been developed, and sometimes chosen, by the person himself or other persons associated with his history. These meanings, however, are not subjective in the sense that they are enclosed within the mind. They originate within the person. But they are also objective and pervade the whole *Lebenswelt,* which is always open to further meaning. The most basic of these meanings are what we now call "values." If we can see some value in a human act, we can see some sense in it. That which is entirely irrelevant to value is meaningless.

Thus the uninterpreted universe of science, as it is first presented to us in abstraction from human care, is meaningless. This universe is factual but without meaning; the human world is ordered by meaning directed to an ultimate value. Any value may come to function in this way. Thus it is possible for the businessman, even though he pays lip service to "higher" values, to regard all regions, activities, and institutions from the standpoint of money-getting, and thus to exist in what we may call a money-making world. Similarly it is possible for the invalid, as well as those who are relatively sound, to regard everything from the standpoint of health, and thus to exist in what we may call a health-getting world. If this is more than an affectation, such world structure will be indicated in the order of his immediate life field, in his conversation, and even in his perceptual and muscular habits.

My lived body is the center of my world, and it contains the general outline of this world already inscribed in my muscles, nerves, and senses. As Merleau-Ponty has pointed out,[1] I already possess in my visual organs the general patterns of all that I will ever be able to see. A thing is not seen by the eye alone but by my bodily behavior toward it, and many of the more important things are already understood in this way before we reflect upon them. My world is ordered with respect to that which I care about most, and this care will be reflected in my body and its attitudes to surrounding objects.

[1] M. Merleau-Ponty, *Phénoménologie de la perception* (Paris: Gallimard, 1945), p. 369.

These objects lie within certain regions—a kitchen, a library, a street, or a market place which fall into a world order or way of life. The objects within each region are either lying around, or are in different places determined by this same order of fitness-for. For the most part, this value order is taken for granted and unnoticed. But when something goes wrong, or when something is lacking, it may suddenly leap into view. This order is not added on to the independent things by subjective value judgments, as the objectivist thinks, for it is actually prior to these things. Thus I cannot get my bearings in a strange room I have just entered by looking at one object after another, and then adding them together. I must first discover what kind of a room it is as a whole, before I can understand the places of these objects. Furthermore I can come to understand a region only by first grasping to some degree of clarity the order of my world as a whole.

Each individual is capable of organizing an eccentric world of his own in terms of his chosen scheme of values. But there are certain structures, like space and time, which will necessarily be found in any world, no matter how eccentric. Thus he himself, together with all the objects of his care, will be carried along in the flow of world time, but his life will not necessarily run off moment by moment like a process in world time. Through his human temporality he may project a future ahead of himself, retain his past, and hold them together in a peculiar integrity that no mere process can achieve. In terms of his lived time, the flux of events will not proceed at an even rate, but will be measured by his care.

The perceived space in which he lives will be very different from geometric space where all points are alike, and where distances are computed by measuring rods. His lived space, on the other hand, is filled with regions and places that are pervaded by human meaning. His body is the center of this human space, and is surrounded by objects at hand for use. He is removed from these things not only by physical distance but also by his effort and care. Thus the very same geometric distance that is only a step for a healthy man may be quite far for a cripple, and a long trip to a friend who is far away may be much shorter than the walk to a dreaded examination.

Many regions which have been established by common consent are characteristic of a given culture. These are concerned with basic, material needs for food and shelter that must be satisfied in some way which for a long time varied from culture to culture. But the need for food has now brought forth techniques of farming and animal husbandry with recognized regions and organized modes of care employing instruments of different kinds.

By means of these instruments, a common living space has been established within each human culture, made up of a complex network of interdependent regions and institutional modes of action. Each region has its own places and times, and in these places, at these times, its own artifacts are ready for use. This value relation of being-for pervades the whole, common living space, connecting not only the artifacts of a given region with their appropriate uses, but one whole region with its use by another region, as the articles produced by industry are used by the market for distribution. This value structure culminates in a final object of ultimate concern to which all other areas and regions are subordinated. This last *for the sake of which* determines the whole direction of life in a human culture or in a single, individual world. These value relations are not subjective in the sense of being private to the individual. They pervade the whole, common living space, and constitute its very being. We are constantly engaged in getting our bearings with respect to this world structure. Hence elaborate systems of signs have been devised in every region, like traffic signals on the streets, to give us this necessary orientation. The world with its value structure is constantly proceeding, and we must make our way through it, if we are to exist.

Finally in the third place, the *Lebenswelt* is marked by the experience of transcendence. Here we must remember that while the global meanings that order and pervade the world of man originate, at least in part, from the individual human agent, the things and persons that make up the world are completely independent of him, and have an existence of their own. This alien existence is inexhaustibly rich, and always transcends such knowledge as I obtain. In fact, this resistance to my knowledge is one of the chief marks of what I call *real things* as over against imaginary constructions. The encounter with any actual thing or person always gives me this sense of what transcends my knowledge, though not necessarily my being in its entirety. In certain feelings like that of the strange and uncanny, and in certain objects, like those we refer to as *holy,* we encounter a radical transcendence of this kind, something mysterious beyond my world, something terrible as well as fascinating that threatens as well as appeals. It is quite evident that there is no human culture or civilization where they are totally unknown.

There are inner, self-conscious pathways to transcendence, and objective pathways as well. We may be led toward it by concentrating on our self-conscious meanings, choices, and feelings, or by noting the checks of objective reason, or by confronting symbolic phenomena such as the holy. They bring us before an ultimate horizon of mystery that encompasses every region of intrinsic value which is capable of an inclusive point of view, such as "the world" of art, and the life-space of a human culture. But this last horizon encompasses the world of the free individual, however it may be organized. It is because I have glimpsed this horizon that I recognize my world, the other man's world, the world of culture, and all other human worlds, no matter how far-reaching, as being only human views of *the* world and within *the* world that transcends them all. This is why in the last analysis, in spite of the vast diversity of historic worlds, and in spite of the conflicting worlds of any given period, we all recognize *the* world as one. This unity is a mystery, and yet also a hard, resistant fact.

There is, of course, a rival world, with no place for self-awareness, global meaning, or transcendence, which claims nevertheless to be all inclusive and coherent. This is the objective world of science, now defended by empiricism, positivism, certain forms of naturalism, and other points of view as the last and most inclusive horizon.

3. *The War of the Worlds*

Each world claims to include and to encompass the other within itself. These opposed claims cannot be reconciled as they stand. This is a basic philosophic issue of our time, perhaps the most basic we are facing. It calls for a critical decision on the part of every individual who does not merely wish to drift, and ultimately on the part of our Western culture as a whole. Much will depend on how this decision is made.

As I have already suggested, this war of the worlds, as we may call it, has been proceeding in different ways throughout the whole history of our Western culture since its origins in ancient Greece. It was involved in the struggle between what Nietzsche called the Apollonian and Dionysian elements in Greek culture, in the conflict between the Aristotelian and Augustinian traditions of the Middle Ages, and in the long debates of modern thought between realism and idealism. In our own time, this issue has been raised by objective science and technology on the one side and the recent discovery of the *Lebenswelt* on the other. In philosophy, we are confronted with a world-wide debate with positivists, naturalists, and logical empiricists on the one hand, and phenomenologists and analysts of ordinary language on the other. This is not a conflict between two technical theories or points of view. It is a war of two worlds, each claiming to include and envelop the other.

Which world is the broader horizon?

Which claim is nearer the truth?

Each one of us must face these questions and answer them as best he can. Out of these individual answers will come the decision of our Western culture, which must also give its answer in the end. On this answer will depend our way of life, our way of understanding, and many other things. In the history of Western thought as a whole, objectivism has been on the winning side of this struggle. Modern positivism and scientism are the last expression of this great tradition, and their defense of the all-inclusive claims of the scientific universe are very strong.

But the objectivist attempts to discredit and reduce such distinctive features of the *Lebenswelt* as self-consciousness, global meaning, and transcendence are unconvincing and dogmatic, being contrary to the true spirit of empiricism. The scientist himself is always aware of his own operations and reflections, though his method gives him no access to this lived awareness which is not an object of any kind. To understand this, another phenomenological method is required.

It is true that a total world view, with its constitutive, global meanings, can be objectively studied by such a science as anthropology (as the world of the Navajo, the Hindu world, etc.). But something essential is lost in this approach. The lived world is fitted into another horizon quite foreign to itself, the horizon of this science. It becomes simply one object among other objects, and loses the very ultimacy and ambiguity which belong to it as the last horizon of lived existence. This may be called by the same name. But it is something else quite different from the world of engaged existence.

Finally, transcendence is manifested to us in many ways in the world of lived experience. There is no known culture where this element of mystery is unrecognized. Like other world facts, it is neither objective nor subjective, but transcends these traditional categories in a peculiarly evident way. To deny such a ubiquitous phenomenon, or to reduce it to the level of a mere "subjective" appearance, is to follow an a priori prejudice rather than the evidence as it actually shows itself to be.

In the light of this evidence, Christian philosophy will recognize the ultimate priority of the life-world. The vast city of science belongs within the life-world, having grown out of it and within it by a long historical development which is now fairly well known and can be clearly traced. Scientists inhabit the very same world as the rest of us. They are born in our hospitals, educated in our schools, walk our streets, and participate in our common life. Their buildings, laboratories, and machines are well marked regions and places in our living space. Their theories, experiments, and operations occur in our ecstatic time, for science certainly has a past and a future.

The so-called scientific universe, which is constantly being confirmed and reconstructed within these regions, is not an ultimate horizon. It is rather a very important but abstract perspective on certain things in the *Lebenswelt*. It regards all entities within the world, including man, and even the world itself, from a detached, factual point of view. Then by its peculiar hypothetico-deductive method, it discovers the facts about all these entities, even the facts about human meanings, after they have relapsed into a dead and *ex-post facto* condition. This perspective has a very accurate and wide-ranging revealing power. There is nothing, indeed, on which it cannot shed a certain kind of light. The development of this objective perspective has been a vitally important phase of our Western cultural history which has transformed the human world and our whole way of life. It has given us a remarkable mastery over concrete objects of the *Lebenswelt,* and has also enormously extended and refined the hazy knowledge of objective detail to which our unaided powers are limited. But the concrete world can never be fitted into this objective universe. It is precisely the contrary which is true. This entire universe, its constitutive acts, together with all its objects, must ultimately be understood in terms of the *Lebenswelt* which is the wider and richer horizon.

4. *A Christian Approach to First Philosophy*

I am not, of course, suggesting that this work of describing and analyzing the world of concrete experience is the only task of philosophy. I believe that this task is of central importance, and should bring philosophers into close touch with other disciplines. This interest in the world of everyday existence should act as a bond linking the members of a faculty together in a common task to which all can contribute. Philosophy has an important role to play in this enterprise. But this by no means exhausts its functions. In describing the phenomena of the *Lebenswelt,* certain basic notions will be encountered whose clarification involves overarching speculation and interpretation of the kind traditionally referred to as ontology or metaphysics. For example: What is being? What is meaning? What is truth? What is transcendence? And why is it that in spite of the diversity that leads us to speak of *my* world, *your* world, the *Western* world etc., we nevertheless all recognize that *the* world is one? These questions are, of course, the peculiar province of philosophy, and they bring us face to face with basic limitations of the human intellect, as the history of the subject makes abundantly clear.

Basic philosophy—let us call it ontology—should neither be neglected nor should it be semicanonized in the form of a fixed, dogmatic system. The approach of the Christian philosopher should be open and free, but not relativistic. The student should be warned against oversimplified versions of the notion of truth, and the dogmatic misuse that has been made of the statement: *the truth is one.* This may be true of God. But it is not true of men. We are surrounded by many regions of diversified being, each one of which transcends our powers of understanding. Hence the term *truth* is not univocal, and the human truth to which we have access is not one. There is the truth of faith, philosophic truth, scientific truth, aesthetic truth, existential truth, trivial truth, etc., each with its own modes and norms. In basic philosophy, we have access to a certain kind of truth, in spite of the feebleness of the human mind.

This truth, however, is always partial and subject to falsity. We are now able to see that the metaphysical tradition of the West, which goes back to Plato, is involved in such partialities and falsities. Instead of directing its attention to the human light of understanding in its actual operations, it has adequately focused only the objects illumined by this light, beings rather than being itself. It has claimed to have access to a divinely grounded reason capable of detaching itself from personal existence and the *Lebenswelt.* From such a worldless position, this reason has then been supposed to be capable of grasping the timeless essence of man, and the essences of other things, to calculate about these things, and thus to win mastery over them for achieving our own purposes (cf. Chapter VI).

Instead of trying more humbly simply to understand itself and its position in the moving world of history, the classical tradition in metaphysics has tried to construct vast explanatory theories of Divine premotion and causation which, as A. A. Vogel has shown in his recent book,[2] not only fail to do justice to human freedom, but also to that active dynamism of physical nature which is now well known to us. Action and passion are not categories or essences, as he so clearly shows. To use Aristotelian language, they transcend all *genera* and *species,* and belong to the creative order of existence.

Its conception of an empty, worldless reason has led this tradition to separate itself artificially not only from the so-called practical life of man, but also from the life of faith in such a way as to make the Augustinian conception of a Christian philosophy impossible.

Finally its view of truth as timeless has led it to view its own widely divergent constructions in each case as a closed system not open to further review on basic points, and, therefore, as something that should end the history of thought. But this history has still gone on, as we now well know. In our historic situation here and now, these traditional theses are no longer open. Hence the Christian philosopher will reject them and will devote himself to the new way of thought that is coming into being around us. I do not know precisely what it will be. But from the nature of this history, about which I do know something, and which I have tried to suggest to you, I believe and hope that it will have the following features.

As over against traditional metaphysics, this new Christian philosophy will try to focus its attention on the light which illumines rather than on the things illumined, on being itself rather than on beings. It will be acutely conscious of the limited, human existence which is responsible for all the works of man, including those of the so-called reason.

[2] Cf. A. A. Vogel, *Reality, Reason, and Religion* (New York: Morehouse Gorham, 1957), pp. 118 ff.

The Christian philosopher will make no claim to a worldless detachment from the human condition but will philosophize as a human person in the world, and out of his concrete situation in history. Abandoning the traditional attempt to identify the fixed, timeless essence of human nature, this philosophy will make no effort to calculate means of self-mastery from a position outside history. Recognizing freedom as a distinctive mark of human existence, the new philosophy will have a clear understanding of its limits. Recognizing that value judgments are involved in all intellectual decisions, it will follow Augustinian thought in refusing to separate the so-called theoretical from the practical, and reason from faith, but will probably go much farther.

Knowing well that its world is enveloped by the mystery of transcendence, and abandoning the notion that knowledge is power, it will seek rather to understand than to explain. Rejecting the traditional conception of a timeless truth, it will be no more hospitable toward what is now called *historicism* and *relativism*. Having access only to a human truth that grows and declines with history, it will be ever open to foundational questioning of its basic meanings, and to new perspectives and reinterpretations.

This, of course, is only a sketch. But it may convey some sense of the philosophic atmosphere that is now developing around us. Such an atmosphere would be open to the faith, and in it I believe that in our time a genuinely Christian philosophy might be worked out, quite free from the sweeping claims of traditional intellectualism. Such a philosophy, with its eyes on the gospel, might work out a coherent interpretation of the present world which did full justice to the available secular evidence. Everything possible should be done to lead the student in this direction. But such an interpretation can never be logically deduced from self-evident premises. If we had any access to first principles of this kind, the history of Western thought would have ended long ago. At certain key points decisions must be made. The student is free. And his freedom must be respected.

5. How Should Christian Philosophy be Taught?

What method should be used in such instruction? Should it be a historical approach, as it is still called, which usually leads to relativism, or a so-called systematic approach, which usually ends in dogmatism? As we all know, philosophy courses are at present classified in this strange way. From some experience I know, as we all probably know, how thoroughly artificial and misleading it is. Even in the most systematic course, the students must read something. And no matter how recent this may be, it now belongs to history. We seem to think that a text gets to be more historical the *older* it is. But this is a strange delusion. Every text whatsoever, the teacher, and the students themselves are historical in their very being. But this history is not yet finished. Nor is the thought expressed in any historical text, no matter how ancient, over and gone. It is not over and gone, because it never was all there. Hence it cannot be understood without living exegesis and criticism. In this sense, every so-called historical course is actually systematic.

I suggest, therefore, that the Christian approach to basic philosophy should be neither what is now called historical nor systematic. I believe that all students should be exposed to this kind of discipline, but that they should be carefully prepared. The student should already know something of the human *Lebenswelt,* and of its basic existential structures. He should already know that the order and meaning of this world rests in large part upon human decision either social and/or personal. He should know that, disagreeable and difficult as these decisions may be, they are an unavoidable necessity from which no person and no culture can ever escape.[3] He should be told that basic philosophy is the attempt to exercise this human freedom in a disciplined way so that it may be constantly illumined and maintained. He should then be told that the history of Western philosophy is the history of the exercise of this disciplined freedom, a history in which he himself is involved, whether he likes it or not.

In studying this history, he will, therefore, be confronted with radically different world orders, in fact with radically different worlds, worked out with precision and care by great thinkers of the West, worlds in which each in his own way has found it possible to think and exist. No one of these gives a complete and final answer to ultimate problems which can be fully confirmed by available evidence. Each of them contains moments of speculation, and is confronted with unsolved problems and mysteries. And yet no one of them is without its germ of human truth. The student will then be told that the aim of the course is to stir him to serious reflection on himself and his world, in order that his own ultimate decisions may be enlightened and responsible rather than slavish and blind.

These suggestions may seem novel, as I believe they are. But we are facing a novel and critical situation in our history which, in my opinion, demands novel modes of approach. Our age has become acutely self-conscious and suspicious of the more than human claims of any human discipline or institution. This wide-spread sense of the historicity of man and of his all too human world is easily interpreted in terms of that historicism which simply abandons the notion of truth, and which has led whole nations and peoples into a cultural chaos demanding tyranny as the only orderly solution. A program of this sort might perform a service to

[3] Cf. W. James, *The Will to Believe and Other Essays* (New York: Longmans, 1897), pp. 214–215.

secular education in showing that while timeless truth is inaccessible, we can still find a growing, human truth in the changing human world of man. It might also show to living men that the Christian faith requires no sacrifice of the intellect either in the form of a gross irrationalism or in that of an uncritical acceptance of a dogmatic system.

This, of course, is only the expression of a hope, though I believe not altogether groundless. In the broken world around us, a strange and radically novel style of human reflection is now beginning to emerge. As I have tried to suggest, this mode of philosophizing, in one of its more influential phases, took its origin more than a hundred years ago in an effort to bring certain long neglected implications of themes in the New Testament to bear on the bitter problems of modern life. Since that time, this way of thinking has shown itself to be amazingly fruitful, and also relevant to the situation of our time. This way of thinking is radically finite, radically human, radically open, and radically free. Out of it there might spring for the first time in our history, such a genuinely Christian philosophy as I have tried to suggest.

Such a philosophy has never been worked out before. Therefore I have had to resort to suggestion rather than exposition. I do not know what the substance of such a philosophy would be. But I have tried to say something about its general nature and method. I have referred to Kierkegaard as an example of such indirect procedure, and have suggested that some of the phenomenological insights into the human *Lebenswelt* resulting from this procedure will be included within it. In connection with the basic questions of meaning, I have made certain negative statements, and have pointed to a mode of approach. I have also said something about the way in which a Christian philosophy should be expressed and taught.

Having now examined the method and the general content of Christian philosophy, we shall now direct our attention to one of its major concerns for a more thorough exploration—Christian ethics and social philosophy.

Chapter Six

CHRISTIAN ETHICS

According to an age-old tradition still expressed in our curricula, ethics is one subject among other branches of philosophy from which it can be clearly marked off. Other disciplines are concerned with God and the world. This discipline is concerned with man. But here another sharp distinction must be made. There are various theoretical sciences of man which study various aspects of human nature from a purely objective and detached point of view. Ethics, however, is a practical discipline which rests on theory only for its general understanding of human nature and the end determined by this nature. With this goal in mind, the ethicist can determine the necessary means, and can show the student how to calculate his way to happiness and self-realization.

This tradition has now been subjected to a basic criticism in the light of which each of these assumptions seems extremely dubious. Human freedom and decision cannot be restricted to a certain region in a universe already fixed and established that can be simply registered by a purely theoretical reason apart from all choice. The world in which we exist is relative to man, and not yet fixed and finished. The way in which we understand this world is not a passive registration of the past but a determination of the world of the future. Freedom is at work in the field of theory as well as in the world of practice. We can no longer hide from ourselves the fact that decisions must be made even in such abstract disciplines as metaphysics, as it has been called, and logic. This does not imply a voluntarism in which theory is reduced to practice, nor a one-sided intellectualism in which practice is governed and controlled by theory. It means rather that we have at last penetrated to an active and self-revealing existence in the world, which underlies both what we call theory and what we call practice.

The task of understanding this existence can no longer be allotted to such special disciplines as ethics or metaphysics. It is a task which belongs to existence itself, and requires all the resources of philosophy. The philosopher cannot get outside history to gaze upon it and to discover its natural end. He must work as he lives and devote himself, so far as he can, to revealing his own situation and the lasting structures of this history. The final end may be guessed. But it cannot be demonstrated. As long as men are alive, the end will remain in question. The traditional end of happiness can be questioned. Indeed it has been questioned by Christian faith. The whole style of rational calculation for realization has been questioned, and must be questioned. The ultimate end of man may rather lie in the expression of freedom, and the suffering that follows in its train. This may require a calculation not so much for getting as for giving—a new style of life and a new mode of thought quite opposed to that which has been developed and cultivated in the dominant core of our Western tradition. Let us now turn to a study of this contrast.

Since our existence is historical, we must begin from what we have been and now are. So let us ask ourselves about that ethics of eudaimonism which has dominated the history of ethical thought in the West. What is its nature? and what is its world? Does it apply to the free, human person? Can it legislate to him as it does to the state? If not, where then does it apply? In connection with these questions, we must remember that he who is to give must exist as a realized person, and must have something to give. After this examination of traditional ethics, let us then turn to Christian ethics. What is its nature and what is its world? How does it compare with that objective morality of eudaimonism which must control social policy?

1. *The Ethics of Self-Realization*

This is the ethics of Western rationalism. In fact every influential ethics that has been formulated in our intellectual history is some version of self-realization. Ethics itself is a special, rational discipline subject to objective analysis and calculation. To act morally is to act in accordance with reason, and to overcome feeling, passion, and every other subjective impulse arising from the lower depths of human nature. Such action is also in accordance with the nature of things, and embraces every human value. Freedom itself is identified with rational choice and behavior. The person is viewed as a substantial self, endowed with definite properties and powers, which occupies a fixed position in the cosmic order. This self is subject to certain normative laws which guide all moral conduct and which can be understood in exactly the same sense by all individuals wherever and whoever they may be. Such reflection is, therefore, eminently social and objective. So far as an individual thinks morally, he abstracts from everything that is distinctive and peculiar to himself, and takes the position of a pure, observing mind which is free from any special bias. From this worldless point of view, which is the same for all rational beings, he regards himself objectively as a part of the social whole to which he belongs.

The aim of such moral reflection is first of all to work out a sound definition of the moral end, based on a true account of human nature and its properties. After this, the rules which must be followed by every man if he is to realize this final end must be clearly formulated. Finally, after he has been properly conditioned and habituated, the individual must be inspired by images and examples of the good life and taught how to apply the universal laws of ethics to his own particular case.

This dominant pattern can be found in classical hedonism; the eudaimonism of Plato, Aristotle, and the Stoics; in the modern idealistic ethics of self-realization and the various forms of utilitarianism. Variations are found in the definition of the final good, and in the various laws and virtues which follow from this. But the basic pattern remains.

This is true even of ethical relativism, which doubts the existence of a single good which is the same for all. But it has not doubted the ability of each individual and state to determine its own good for itself, and to calculate for its own apparent self-interest. It is true that Kant partially broke with this pattern in denying that the free person could be understood as an object in the phenomenal world, and that the final good could be empirically demonstrated. But he still held that the person could be understood as a noumenal reason laying down universal laws for itself, leading to a final *summum bonum* which might be realized in an after-life. So the basic pattern remains intact.

In this pattern, we may distinguish five major aspects: objective calculation, universal law, self-centeredness, self-realization through works, and retrospection. Let us now consider these one by one with some care.

Objective Calculation

According to the traditional conception, moral decision is determined by a process of so-called deliberation which occurs within the individual person who is already located within a fixed world frame. Deliberation presupposes an objective understanding of the laws of nature and the natural consequences of different kinds of act, as well as a grasp of the final end which must be already understood theoretically before the process can begin. As Aristotle tersely put it: We deliberate about means only, not about ends. In such practical reflection on ourselves, we bring alternative courses of action before our minds objectively. Then we envisage the alternative consequences to be realized in each case, and the different attending values and disvalues. In this process of self-examination, any value to be realized, or any disvalue to be avoided, constitutes a motive. When we have finally discovered the action which will bring us closest to the final end, and for which there is seen to be the strongest rational motive, this act is singled out and finally chosen. Unless we have lost control of ourselves, this act will then be performed. If the real end of man has been properly determined, and if we have made no mistake in our calculations, such an act will be rational, virtuous, and free.

It is, of course, assumed that everything about the human act, including its end and the way in which it is to be carried out, can be brought before the mind as an object of deliberation without any distortion or loss. It is also assumed that the self-consciousness with which the act must be performed, if it is to be truly virtuous, can be achieved in this same objective way. Thus all my actual motives before the act, as well as the act itself, can be objectively envisaged by a detached reason which watches them and records them exactly as they are. Even more, this reason, working with a peculiar kind of desire, can order these motives by reflection, bring them into act through choice, and then guide them to their natural end. Finally, it can reflect upon the ultimate result and judge its merit or demerit.

There is no question that processes of this sort do occur, especially in connection with the determination of social policy. Here various contrary moving interests are objectively envisaged and expressed. Then means are devised by which the greatest number can be realized to the maximum degree, and the resulting compromise is put into effect under the rational control of the executive agency. But grave questions can be raised as to whether this description does justice to the basic decisions of the free, human person. One we have already suggested. Can personal understanding be restricted merely to acts within a fixed world framework? Does it not also affect the world order itself? But other questions also arise. Can my intentions be really inclosed within a subjective container? Do they not rather extend to the farthest limits of my world, and pervade it as a whole? Does the final end lie completely beyond the range of human freedom? Can we seriously accept the Aristotelian doctrine that we deliberate about the means only, and never about the end? Does not the very history of ethics refute this dogma in no uncertain terms?

Other questions may be raised concerning my capacity to bring the whole of my being before the mind as an object with no distortion or loss. Is it not true that my act, in being performed, includes "subjective" factors that cannot be objectified? Granted that the nature of the act may be gazed at and clearly distinguished from other kinds, is this true of the act itself and the way in which it is performed, with freedom, let us say, or ultimate concern, or purity of intent? Granted that these terms can be understood, can they be brought before the mind as objects? Or do they not require another mode of participative understanding? I certainly possess some grasp of my total being. But how can I ever gaze upon this as an object? How can the *I* that is gazing be included in the *I* that is object?

Can we then avoid concluding that the traditional kind of deliberation is concerned only with subordinate decisions concerning partial aspects of our being, and that the basic choices, which affect our whole existence in the world, must be made in another way, in an entirely different context? Is it not clear that those who think that their basic way of life has been rationally determined by a panoply of objective reasons and motives are suffering from a serious delusion? By the time they start deliberating in this way, their basic reasons and motives have already been chosen by a deeper and more primordial mode of choice. Much of what is called *rational delibera-*

tion by the individual is really only a hollow rationalization and a sham. The analysis of this subordinate process sheds no real light on the way in which basic decisions are really made.

Universal Law

Traditional ethics has been based upon universal laws or principles which can be understood in the very same way by different minds. This already says something about the act of understanding, as well as about what is understood. Each of these is abstract and partial. In order to hold good for all individuals, the law that is understood must be based on observed similarities in human structure. Hence to arrive at such principles we must abstract in the first place from subjective factors which cannot be "observed." Then in the second place, we must also abstract from individual differences that can be observed in these objects in order to focus on common needs and tendencies. What emerges, therefore, is an abstract, objective principle, what must be done by man in general to attain the universal good for man as such.

We may note a similar abstractness in the mode of understanding. If the moral law is to apply to all men, it must apply to me, for there can be no exceptions. Hence I must regard myself also as an object, and thus become separated from myself, for that which reflects cannot be identified with that which is reflected upon. If it is to gain an adequate view of my needs and interests, it must become detached from them. But such a detached, observing mind will be abstract and, therefore, partial, for surely my needs and interests belong to me. We may summarize this by saying that *a law is an abstract object of an abstract mode of understanding.*

We must grant, of course, that such a partial mode of apprehension may reveal important facts about both nature and man. Such insights are especially important in the conduct of social affairs in the public world. For unless human groups can agree on government by laws that can command assent, they

will fall into chaos, and government by force will be necessary. But when we are told by the tradition that all questions
of human conduct are to be ultimately decided by an appeal to
moral law, and that the human person is subject to such abstract principles in the same way as the human mass or group,
we may raise certain serious questions concerning both the
object understood and the mode of understanding it.

Can these abstract principles give me adequate guidance
for my concrete existence in my *Lebenswelt?* Granted that
they may legislate to me so far as I am a technician, a learner,
or a citizen, can they legislate in the same way to the whole
of my existence? Can they guide me in exercising that radical
freedom by which I choose to interpret my world in a certain
way? Or do they rather presuppose certain acts of interpretation as already made on a deeper level of understanding? Is it
not clearly at such a deeper level that I must find whatever way
it is by which I understand my personal existence in the world
as a whole? Is it not in the light of some such understanding
that I must decide the basic issues confronting me in my situation in history, and work out my basic meanings, together with
the thoughts and acts in my world that only I can do?

The Self as World Center

The living of human life is a process of becoming. Self-
realization ethics, of course, recognizes this fact. But it tries to
inclose this process within a structure of fixed essences. The
self is an enduring substance which maintains certain essential
properties from beginning to end. If the nation is to endure, it
must maintain the same constitution which defines its purposes and powers. Its existence is to be understood in terms of
these purposes which are either realized by the attainment of
peace and order, or frustrated by internal and external struggle and disintegration. At birth the human self is endowed
with a nature that determines certain possible ways of acting
that may or may not be realized. The self is not these possibil-

ities. Its aim, in fact, is to eliminate them by realization. As long as it is incomplete, it has them in a latent state. But whether or not they are actualized, the essential self remains the same.

Thus in the Aristotelian tradition, virtues and vices are accidents. Whatever I do, I remain essentially what I am. To realize a capacity is to achieve a value. But this does not affect its nature. The self in its potential state is the same as the realized self. To rest in this state of determinate actuality is good. To be on the way is to be separated from the good. Hence the sharp separation of means from ends. The process of arriving is a mere means that is negative or neutral in value. Only rest in realization at the end has positive value. This is the source of human meaning.

Such an ethics is centered in human selves. Every social policy must be regarded from the point of view of how far it may realize the established purposes of the group. Individual ethics also is oriented toward the notion of self-realization. There is no place for essential growth and creativity. Every moral act, including sacrifice, is viewed as the actualization of some determinate tendency already there in potency. Divine Grace itself is understood as a last level of realization which completes and perfects a nature that is present from the very start.

This self-centered pattern underlies ancient and medieval eudaimonism as well as modern idealistic ethics and utilitarianism. Indeed it is fair to say that Western ethics is the history of variations on this theme. This is enough to show that it represents a basic trend of objectivist thought. When man is regarded from the outside in this way, he looks like a thing, and his life becomes a process of realization. Indeed, it is hard to see any other way of regarding the human group, whose very being, as we shall see, is objective (Chapter VIII). But personal existence has to be lived from the inside, and this existence can be explored by poetry and literature, and is open to historical and philosophical analysis. In the light of such knowledge as we now possess, serious questions may be raised as to whether the traditional thing categories do justice to this existential becoming.

For example, can the acts of an existing person be regarded as mere accidents which may be added or subtracted from a fixed self that remains essentially unaffected? Is it not rather the case that this self grows and declines in history? Do the existential possibilities lie outside the person himself? Or is he rather always constituted, in his very being, by such possibilities, and by the way in which he holds them? Can he ever be conceived in a finished or realized state? Or is he essentially unfinished and incomplete? As long as he lives, is he ever found to be resting at a stable end? Or is every end simply a novel situation? Can we then accept that sharp separation of means from end which is characteristic of the Western tradition? Is positive value to be identified with the realization of a changeless state? Or is it to be found rather in the becoming, and more especially in certain modes of becoming? Do not creative acts sometimes occur which found new possibilities not already present? If so, they cannot be subsumed under the category of self-realization.

Another alternative looms on the scene. Is the existing person not capable of giving as well as of realizing himself? Does this not enable us to understand Grace in a more Biblical manner as not so much a completion of nature as a creative self-sacrifice in which my life becomes oriented toward an other transcending me?

Works

There is no doubt that a large part of our activity consists in works which we first consider as possibilities in relation to a standard of some kind held before the mind. After a process of deliberation, we then choose and finally carry them out, or realize them in the world with more or less success. So far as

I regard this work as an object, it is not I, for I am regarding it from the outside. When I choose to carry out this work, I am choosing to have it as a possession, not myself. As I watch over the work in performing it, I am not in it with the whole of my being. I am rather watching it as I perform it, standing closely by its side. It is not I but my work, my function, that I am performing. I may become so intensely absorbed in it as to forget myself. We speak of those who lose themselves in their work. But this is only an approximating mode of speech. If they were to be completely lost, they would cease to be human, and would become a set of functions. But this is abnormal and rare. Absorbed they may be. But they are still there watching and doing their work, and may be easily recalled.

This duality still remains when the work is finished. It is not I myself but my work which I have produced, and for which I am responsible. Therefore I can regard it from the outside, and compare it with an objective norm accessible to everyone. If it departs from the norm, I can be criticized and blamed. On the other hand, if it agrees, I can claim credit and deserve reward. Self-realization is a process of this kind that can be checked by objective norms accessible to all. I can observe myself from the outside and can compare this self with an ideal or realized self as a norm. If I fall short, I am guilty. In so far as I agree, I am realized and, therefore, deserve merit.

This scheme underlies the most influential ethical systems that have been devised in the West. But it is subject to certain questions such as the following. Granted that much of my life is devoted to works which are decided upon by a process of objective deliberation, this does not explain how I come to myself. I cannot deliberate about this self from the outside, for this is the self that deliberates. How then do I decide to be or not to be myself? What kind of decisions are these? And what is this becoming?

It cannot consist of works from which I can detach myself,

but rather of acts that constitute my inner being. What sort of acts are these? They cannot be observed by any kind of introspection. How then are they known? When they are finished I do not *have* them as possessions. I *am* them. Hence I cannot gaze upon them to compare them with objective norms accessible to all. How then can I claim credit for the acts that I perform with full integrity, and that constitute my personal being? How can I judge that I myself am guilty?

An answer to these questions is presupposed by the ethics of self-realization. For how can I understand the works that are mine if I know nothing of myself? These questions point to another, deeper ethics back of objective works, and norms, and merits. This is the ethics of my own existence in its full integrity. What kind of an ethics is this?

The Priority of the Past

An ethics of realization necessarily looks back to the already given nature, or self, that is to be realized. This original nature is endowed with fixed structures which determine the general character of the human end and the changeless laws that must be followed if this end is to be attained. Determinism, of course, is rejected. It is only the general nature of the end which is fixed in advance, and which leaves the way open for an indefinite variety of exemplifications. But any view of the end that is basically different is a misconception which must lead to the loss of freedom. Genuine freedom is to be realized only within a pattern already established by the human essence as it is, and the world order to which this essence belongs, as these can be registered by objective reason. In this sense, we can say that the moral future is already determined by structures realized in the past. Any radical exercise of freedom which violates natural law, or the dialectic of world history, will only destroy itself. Even Grace itself must remain within the limits prescribed by this objective nature.

These implications of self-realization ethics are also subject to doubt. For example, one may wonder whether the critical passage we have considered (Chapter I) from mythical, prehistorical society to the kind of civilization which supports personal freedom and the exercise of reason can be dismissed as a mere accidental change which left man essentially as he was before. In reading the history of philosophy in the West, one may also wonder whether radically different world views, involving radically different conceptions of the human end, have not been cogently and coherently formulated, and whether some of these, at least, have not had a marked effect on our actual history.

It is now time for us to bring Christian ethics into focus, and to ask whether it is not basically different from those utilitarian modes of thought which have dominated our secular history. Such reflections may lead us to ask if, in addition to the many examples where ways of regarding the past have evidently determined ways of regarding the future, there are not other cases where new ways of regarding the future have determined new ways of regarding the past. Can freedom be held within the limits of a rational system that is fixed and closed? Can it live and breathe within such a context?

Does not history show us clearly that this mode of thought, when consistently developed, leads rather to a determinism in which true freedom has no place? Can freedom be even conceived with any degree of clarity in such an objective universe? Or does it require an open, historic world of its own with a very different structure? Can freedom be placed within any closed construction of reason which supposedly precedes it? Or is it not rather already involved in the choices underlying such a construction? Is Divine Grace held within the chains of a closed system already established? Or is it capable of transforming nature, and of making all things new?

These questions, I think, open up the possibility of another kind of ethics quite distinct from any version of self-realization. Is Christian ethics of this kind? If so, what is its nature?

And how is it to be understood? Let us now turn to these questions.

2. *Christian Ethics*

If our questions are really relevant, medieval Thomism and modern, liberal Christianity have been quite wrong in interpreting Christian ethics as a special version of self-realization. As a matter of fact, it belongs to an entirely different genus with a radically different world background which is so unfamiliar to us that the problem of finding language adequate to express it is quite serious. In spite of its vagueness, a negative method of contrast would seem to be advisable. Hence in order to get some grasp of it as a whole, let us compare it in general with the objective ethics of our rationalist tradition.

First of all, it is not a special discipline that can be allotted a restricted territory over against the other sciences and arts. It is not concerned with an individual substance existing in himself, but with a person existing in a world, involving subjective as well as objective factors. Hence serious feeling and thinking about anything in the world, and especially about the world itself, may be relevant to ethics in this sense. This involves much more than objective calculation about those of my works which may be objectively envisaged. Such thinking is not confined to those aspects of my world which I share with others. It is especially concerned with *I myself* as an existing individual, and with those things that only I can do.

This ethics is not restricted to what I do for myself as I already am, but with what I do with myself as a whole in the light of my death. Hence it includes the possibility of self-giving as well as of self-getting, and of reorienting my world around a center other than myself. It is interested not so much in what I do as in how I do whatever I do, not so much with specific works from which I can detach myself, and for which I can claim credit, as with how I live the whole of my being before transcendence. Finally it is interested in a freedom that can do something more than adjust me to a world that is already fixed and finished. It is rather concerned with that deeper freedom that can affect the whole meaning of the world in which I exist, and which is open to a creative future.

So much for a general sketch. Let us now examine this ethics in further detail and contrast it point for point with the five aspects of realizationism we have just considered.

Objective Calculation vs. Existential Thought

Few ideas have had a more disastrous influence on the course of Western philosophy than that of ethics as a special, practical science with a restricted territory of its own. It has not only deadened the rest of philosophy by removing it from any intimate relation with life as it is lived in the concrete; it has also weakened the conception of freedom, and ethics itself, by isolating it from the range of its most basic decisions and restricting it to a subordinate level of practical calculation which takes the world for granted. We do not calculate objectively about our final ends by the process traditionally named *deliberation*. There is this much truth in the Aristotelian doctrine of means and end. This does not mean, however, that we cannot become concerned with our ends, and have nothing to do with deciding them. What it means is that we do not arrive at such decisions by the process described by Aristotle as deliberation.

This process is not a special phase of our existence clearly marked off from the rest. It is essentially involved with our existence in the world. Hence it is not restricted to certain "personal" objects. It may be concerned with any object or phase of my existence. It does not occur only at well marked and relatively brief intervals of internal reflection. It occurs throughout the whole course of my life, and affects not only my internal attitudes but the structure of my world. Such existential reflection is not limited to the discursive methods of objective "reason." It also makes use of feeling, passion, expressive discourse, and every revealing power to which we have access. This explains the notorious artificiality and woodenness of books on ethics.

The decisions which underlie our way of existing do not terminate a brief interval of calculation at a moment when they switch us on to another track, and then fall into oblivion. They arise gradually through long intervals of time from the depths of our being and, if genuine, are then repeated with constant variations to meet new situations. These self-revealing acts are for the most part unthematized and inarticulate. Nevertheless we understand them in a hazy way, as we understand the world in which we live. This prethematic understanding can be further illumined in the full richness of its biographic and historic detail by literary art and poetry. One can learn infinitely more about the actual exercise of freedom from a discerning novel than from twenty moral text books.

This does not mean, however, that there is no place for the distinctive kind of clarity that comes from phenomenology. The task of this discipline is to distinguish the essential from the accidental, and to reveal with maximum clarity the necessary structures of lived existence, like being-in-the-world, lived space and time, feeling, understanding, and the meaning of historicity. In such ways, it may deepen that self-understanding which is an essential phase of human existence. But this, of course, does not exhaust the functions of philosophy. By a study of the history of philosophic thought, the student may become more clearly aware of radically different interpretations of the world, and may be helped to make choices that are less blind and unstable. Through the critical comparison of these different worlds, he may become clearer about the basic direction of his own existence as a whole, and more ready for that existential communication of self to self which is essential for the endurance of a democratic society where basic decisions are not concealed.

Freedom cannot be placed within an objective frame which is simply accepted without criticism. It cannot be restricted to instrumental choices concerned with objects alone. Such freedom in a frame is really slavery. To be authentic, it must grasp the frame itself as a whole in its subjective as well as its objective aspects. This total understanding comes only through philosophy. Freedom is not license. It is a discipline. And in all these ways philosophy functions as the discipline of freedom.

These existential truths are, of course, accessible to the secular phenomenologist. Since they are clearly suggested in the Biblical literature, they should be even more readily accessible to the Christian philosopher. In this literature there is no sharp separation of the theoretical from the practical, nor the person from his world. Man is understood together with the world he inhabits, whose meaning for him depends upon his choices. Those whose ultimate concern is for mundane things are referred to as *the world*. Practical calculation for given ends is, of course, recognized, but our attention is constantly directed to the whole way of our existing in the world, which is far more important. Thus in the Sermon on the Mount we are warned against being too anxious in our predictions and calculations about the morrow (Mat. 6:30–34), and to the greedy farmer who has filled his bins it is said: "Thou fool, this night will thy life be required of thee" (Luke 12:20). But there is no point in mustering texts.

The Gospel is a call to decision about the whole way of life, and presupposes a corresponding revealing power which, though usually neglected and suppressed, belongs necessarily to the being of man. Otherwise it would not be constantly urged upon us and commanded. This understanding is not restricted to objects which can be brought before the mind. It is a total understanding concerned not only with what we see but with our own inner attitudes and the way in which we see what we see. Thus we are not told not to see the speck in our neighbor's eye—the defects in his vision. We are told to see and understand them. But in order that we may "see clearly" to take out this speck, we must "first take the log out of our own" (Mat. 7:5 R.S.V.). We are here presented with the intentional structure of human knowledge in no uncertain terms. No object is ever passively received in a totally empty mind. It must be understood in a certain way by a certain prior attitude. And these prior attitudes need to be purified.

Hence the Bible is constantly concerned with the original intentions of the human heart. We never grasp objects just as they are in themselves, but only as we already understand them in relation to ourselves. Such a total understanding is always at least dimly with us, and is desperately in need of being clarified. When we have attained some clarity of this kind, we may come to see that our repeated claim to have made a purely rational decision amongst objective motives that are simply there before the mind is a hollow sham. These motives are not simply there. They have already been chosen and weighed by a genuine choice that has welled up from the depths of our existence.

Concerning this existential choice we need more light. But the traditional interpretation of it in terms of a "will" enclosed within an objective frame and hard pressed by alien forces is a rationalization that leads us to determinism. This objective frame is not the field of freedom which is a world of its own—the world of our lived existence.

Universal Law vs. the Existing Person

We must grant that if an individual is going to understand the community in which he lives, he must be able to abstract from his own peculiar ways of thought, and assume the role of a consciousness in general which can regard himself, and anything at all, as anyone would do. Furthermore, if he is to work with others voluntarily, he must be given a common goal which he can understand in terms of common needs and desires and which can be realized by co-operative work. The universal rules which must be followed, if this human end is to be realized, become the moral or natural laws of human realization, or the particular laws of a given community. Every form of social life must exemplify this abstract pattern. Social ethics is necessarily an ethics of self-realization. But when the claim is made by our tradition that the human person, as a part of the group, is also subject in the same way to the very same ethics without further qualification, then, as we have seen, basic questions can be raised. In a later chapter (VII) we shall examine this claim in greater detail. At the present stage of our argument we shall simply reject it, and follow the guidance of our questions in suggesting that personal ethics requires something more than the universal prescriptions of social and moral law.

If personal freedom is to be exercised, certain conditions must first be realized. Persons must be nurtured, educated, and given the opportunities for real choice. These conditions may be objectively defined and prescribed by universal rules which apply to social policy. But they do not apply in the same way to the free person, once he is in existence. They mark the limits of his finite freedom and, therefore, apply to him negatively. No one may injure others, kill them, or misinform them without jeopardizing his existence as a person. These negative principles, however, do not legislate affirmatively to him as they do to the state. They do not prescribe to his freedom; they merely mark off its limits. If he is to be given any helpful guidance, a very different kind of "ethics" is required.

This "ethics" of the person must be affirmative rather than negative. It must give him some light not merely on what he should do as a functionary in realizing some universal end, but on how he should exist in his own unique situation in history. It must understand him as he exists, not in a fixed, objective frame, but in the open horizon of his world, confronting an ambiguous future. It must regard not only his objective properties and capacities but his "subjective" attitudes and intentions as he lives them from the inside. In particular, it must not ask him merely to think of what anyone else should do if anyone were in his situation. This is a pure abstraction. "Anyone" is never in an actual situation. He is! And no other existing person can be himself. In order to help him decide what he should do not with an abstract aspect, but with the whole of his being-in-the-world where he is, it will not be enough to present him with universal laws and principles which apply to situations only in so far as they are the same. His situation is different. Hence he needs more light on what it means to be in a situation, on what it means to be, and on the diverse, alternative ways of interpreting his world that may be open to him. Only by such an "ethics" can he be helped to create those new meanings and acts which may meet his existential need.

Christian ethics, of course, is not the only possibility. But it is an ethics of this kind. It recognizes the human necessity for a universal moral law of self-realization. But it also recognizes the need for something more than the law to fulfil the law. This is because the law must be carried out in the concrete by existing persons with an abstract part of themselves, for the sake of themselves as persons. So the law is made for man, not man for, or under, the law. The Christian Saviour is himself a human person, and against the hopes and wishes of his disciples, is not primarily concerned with social revolution and the abstract pattern of law as such. He is concerned not exclusively with men as members of a social system but with them as persons, exercising their radical freedom in history. Hence he speaks to them as persons, and singles them out one by one. He has come not to build another objective kingdom of this world ruled by law, but another kind of kingdom not of this world—a temple built of individuals of which he is the cornerstone.

This is a kingdom of free persons united not by the bonds of law, which can stifle freedom, but by a sacrificial love which nourishes it, and brings it to perfection. Christian ethics, therefore, is not so much concerned with the abstract law as with the whole person in his concrete situation, not so much with what is done as how it is done—its inner spirit and intention. Its attention is not primarily focused on the general pattern by which human life can be realized. This is taken for granted. Its attention is focused rather on the radical exercise of human freedom. What shall the free individual do with his whole existence once it has been given him? Shall he devote it to further realizations of himself? Or shall he give to something transcending himself? This question brings us to another topic.

Resting and Possessing vs. Becoming and Giving

The ethics of realization is based on the conception of a fixed self, directed toward a determinate goal which underlies all the accidents of its history. This self, like a thing, has certain possibilities which lie beyond its essence. When such a possibility is realized, the self may possess this reality, and then go on from there in a cumulative history. Thus if it is fortunate, it may build one realization on another until it reaches the natural end where it may rest in peace, like a plane that has reached its destination. There is no doubt that human groups have fixed and definable natures and ends of this sort which may be stated in written constitutions that underlie their history. Other social endeavors, like technology and science, have a cumulative history. Like living organisms, most groups, after early turbulent periods of origin and growth, reach a stable condition of balanced change in which they tend to rest. But as we have seen, when we apply this traditional conception to the existing person, certain basic questions arise. To these questions let us now attempt to suggest an answer.

It is true that the person requires certain conditions without which he cannot exist at all. But under these conditions, unlike a group or artifact, his nature and end remain undefined. They are open to choice. Hence the acts of a person are not rightly understood as accidents added to a fixed essence. These acts make him what he is. The person *is* his history. As long as he exists, the person is projected ahead of himself into certain possibilities which make up what we call his *future*. This future is not an accident. It is an essential phase of his being. Furthermore, it cannot be realized. It can only be *held* in certain ways. This future may be forgotten, or evaded, or predicted, or hoped, or feared. Nevertheless as long as we live, it lies before us, and is never realized as an end in which we can rest. The "end" is death, a very different kind of end in which nothing is realized.

When the idea of rest in finite achievement breaks down, the distinction between means and ends goes with it. Any value that is to be found must be found not in distinct achievements, but in the whole becoming—the creation of existence. Two alternatives here confront us. In the first, we are ready to give up the past for the sake of a new future which we ourselves are to create. We may call this *personal sacrifice*, which has been exemplified in such revolutionary figures as Socrates who were able to find a real satisfaction in abandoning the past for a creative possibility. Since satisfaction is rest in a finite achievement, we must recognize this as a kind of realization. But it is not the realization of a self that remains fixed. An old self is really sacrificed. The satisfaction is felt in a *new self* barely born. There is a dialectical discontinuity here that is wholly absent from traditional theories of self-realization. This is a getting only through giving, a realization only in and through a sacrifice that is found in all human creation. Fine as it is, it is subject to the tragic sense, for there is no human creation that can last, and in which we can find final rest. So this leads to the second alternative.

This alternative has abandoned the hope of resting in any

worldly realizations, all of which pass like a wind in the grass. Therefore this is the way of death. Like the way of personal sacrifice it is creative, for in it all things are to become new. It is also a total becoming in which there is no distinction of means and end. But instead of a partial sacrifice to a new human future, there is here a free and total sacrifice to the transcendent. When it occurs, instead of a resting and possessing, we find a total becoming and giving in which no self-realization remains. In this self-abandonment there is an answer to the sense of tragedy. This is the Christian way.

Works vs. Acts

The self of traditional ethics is an objective entity that can be analyzed into works which it produces and judges in terms of universal norms. A human life is built up out of works, like a bridge or a building, and will turn out well or badly, depending on the accuracy of the preceding calculations which guide it to its end. This is, of course, a possible way of life but, as we have seen, there are other alternatives. Hence to give oneself over to self-realization and to calculation about worldly works rests on a prior decision of self-interpretation. What kind of decision is this? And how is it made? It is to these questions that we must now attempt to sketch out an answer.

It is clear that I cannot get outside this self to calculate about it, for this is the very self that I am. These thoughts belong to my being, and I am involved in them. So calculation is out of the question. Furthermore it is clear that my whole existence-in-this-world is at stake, not merely a fragmentary work in a frame already established. The frame itself is in question. Finally I cannot compare this whole being with any fixed norm beyond it, for my world is a normative structure. So the norm itself is precisely the point at issue. Self-revealing activity of this kind usually proceeds sporadically and unthematically over long intervals of time. It cannot be confined to ratiocination alone, but certainly includes feeling, passion, and aspiration as well. Neither can it be reduced to any systematic order. But as we have already suggested, it may be pursued in a disciplined way which shows the following features.

First, it is a mode of revealing thought which is acutely self-conscious all the while it is conscious of objects. Second, it must be aware of the norms it is presupposing. Finally, third, it must be concerned with self-world structure as a whole and with those clashes between divergent world interpretations which occur in what we now call philosophical discourse. So far as our different ways of life are freely chosen in the light of what may be made manifest by disciplined effort, they are guided not by ethical calculation but by this kind of existential thinking. Some general evidence is certainly accessible. Much of this has been brought to light, but never enough to constrain a particular interpretation of the world. Hence any choice that is actually made in concrete history is attended by an element of final risk and uncertainty.

Now let us suppose that such a choice has been made of a total way of existing-in-the-world. How will this be expressed? It cannot be expressed by isolated works which I can calculate and judge from the outside, like my possessions. It can be expressed only in the form of acts in which I am wholly present with my past and with my future. Such an act is not something I have done or produced and for which I am merely responsible. I cannot stand beside it and watch it or possess it, for it is a part of me. How then can I know it? Not by any intentional looking at, or regarding. Only by a non-positional mode of awareness that dwells in the very act as it is first projected, as it proceeds, and as it is held in living remembrance. To express this lived awareness is the task of what is now called phenomenology.

How can I judge this act when it is over? I cannot compare it with an objective norm ultimately justified in terms of human use. This is the way I judge an artifact. It is not in this way that I can take credit for, or blame myself for such acts, since they are myself. It is not something I am judging as fit or unfit for some objective, measurable phase of myself. It is I myself I am judging directly—as fit for what? in terms of what norm beyond myself? Have I any real access, short of faith, to such a norm, beyond the human norms that I myself have already accepted or chosen as the essential core of my world and my existence? When I express my own self-pleasure at my own self-realization, am I then saying any more than that I am in agreement with myself—that I am what I am? My norms fit my norms. Sometimes this is all that is meant.

But usually there is another shade of meaning beyond this reiteration. If I go on to say: What other standard is there? or This is all there is! then the statement ceases to be analytic, and becomes an act of faith in non-transcendence. I believe that the world is equivalent to the world of which I am the center. But in the light of the similar claims of other men, and the pervasive presence of mystery, this assertion is far from being proved. It is an act of faith which can be performed only by the evasion or suppression of other conflicting evidence of guilt. What then of this experience?

How and by what norm can I know that I am guilty? This experience in some form is probably common to all men. Hence the question requires an answer which should take the following form. Existence carries with it a common structure wherever it goes. This structure constitutes an intrinsic norm which to some degree is internally revealed within each human life. This norm is not an essence or possibility to be realized. It is rather a way of existing, a total integrity to be freely chosen and held. If men say they are guilty, this must mean that they are divided against themselves, or have not become themselves.

But this norm, even though it be found in all men, may still be only an absurd accident in world history. To be human is simply to be guilty. This again is only a pessimistic version of humanocentrism. To take this guilt seriously, to believe that I am really guilty before transcendence is an attitude that cannot be proved. This also is an act of faith, but of a very different kind.

The Christian philosopher will be already prepared for these existential truths by the guiding image of his faith. They are all clearly suggested in the New Testament. The Word concerning ultimate things is the proper subject for deliberation. When in the parable it is said to fall among thorns, this means it is choked out by worldly cares and calculations (Mat. 13:22). "By their fruits ye shall know them" (Mat. 7:16). Does this not mean that as the tree is its fruits, so the man is his acts? We have said that we do not gain our deepest understanding of man by gazing at him from the outside, but rather by following his own guiding spirit as it is revealed from the inside. Is not St. Paul suggesting this when he says (I Cor. 2:11): "For what man knoweth the things of a man save the spirit of man which is in him?" We have referred to the important distinction between works and acts, and have pointed out that any merit in the former presupposes a prior merit in the latter which cannot be objectively demonstrated, but which rests on faith. Is this not clearly suggested by the Pauline doctrine of justification by faith? [1]

Priority of the Past vs. Priority of the Future

Self-realization ethics asserts the priority of the past. It must constantly look backwards to a changeless self, or nature, that is already fixed and established. It is this fixed nature that determines the end to be realized. All justifiable hope for the future is based on a memory of the past. This backward-looking hope is found in those versions of natural

[1] Cf. Rom. 3:23–28, and Bultmann's comments, *Theology of the New Testament*, I, 270–285.

law philosophy which have become associated with the Christian tradition of our culture. Sin is here interpreted as the fall from a natural or normal state, once realized in paradise. Moral action and saving Grace are then regarded as the restoration of a pristine Golden Era. This conception is responsible for that stubborn rigidity which has been a marked feature of "Christian" social thought throughout a large part of its history. The meanings which can be correctly apprehended by reason are absolutely determined by a complete objective structure already established and fixed. Any origination of basic meanings can lead only to misconception. The scope of freedom is, therefore, restricted to the devising of novel means for the realization of a pre-established end. But we have seen that these conceptions are subject to serious questions.

These questions point to a radically different ethics based on a priority of the future. This future is bathed in mystery and, therefore, continually open to further creative understanding. This does not mean that lasting truth cannot be discovered. It does mean that such truth is ever open to new perspectives and reinterpretation. This ethics will grant that there are stable human properties, but will deny that they are fixed for all time, and unaffected by the decisions of history. Hence it must be historically oriented. Such an ethics will grant that facts of history condition the present and future, but it will point out that the meaning of these facts depends upon a future which we also share. Hence any justifiable interpretation of the past must rest on an authentic project for the future, and as these projects change, history also must be rewritten. No past period can be understood without an understanding of its (and our) future. Hence the authentic historian must be constantly on the lookout for those real possibilities of man which are worthy of creative repetition. Instead of a backward-looking hope, we may characterize this attitude as a forward-looking historicity. In such an ethics there is a place for the creation of new meanings, since the world is as yet unfinished and its mystery inexhaustible. Freedom does not depend on any fixed frame set up by reason, for reason begins with the question Why? Why is something not otherwise than it is? Such being-open-to-otherness is that freedom which lies at the root of the being of man. And what we still call reason is an expression of this freedom.

The Christian philosopher, looking toward his guiding image, will not be surprised to find that these truths are open to secular investigation, for they are clearly indicated in the literature and traditions of the faith. The idea of the Golden Age is a pagan conception with no foundation in the Bible itself, which is dominated by a forward-looking eschatological hope for a new Heaven and a new earth. In this literature there is no elaboration of a fixed frame of essence in which history is to be enclosed. It is rather the account of a world history which is itself the ultimate horizon in which all other events, ideas, and systems are contained. Finally, this is the history of a human freedom that is unrestricted and unqualified to the highest degree.

We may perhaps understand this more clearly if we reflect for a moment on the meaning of freedom as being-open-to-otherness. It is a capacity for self-transcendence-*to,* which is evident in every major phase of human existence, to the past and the future (not now), *to* other objects in the spatial field around it (not where I am), and *to* being with others (not myself). As we have seen, it is also evident in that other-than-it-is which stirs the quest of reason. Man's being is ecstatic, ever beyond itself. Let us now ask how this being is to be fulfilled? The conditions for its possibility may be realized and possessed. But freedom cannot be realized in this way without destroying it. Any possession to which I cling, whether it be material or personal, merely confirms me in that slavish rest in myself as I am to which Christian thought has given the name of pride. This is the opposite of freedom which cannot be obtained and had by any act of getting.

How then is it to be enacted? What acts are genuinely free?

Acts of giving seem to remain. But these are of many kinds. To give away things or possessions is irrelevant, for this leaves us as we are. It is the self that must be given. Only such an act is self-transcendent and free in its very act. But to what being can the self be given without being taken over and thus reduced to slavery? How is this freedom to be maintained? If we give ourselves over to the possession of things, they obsess us and take us over. The same is true of ideals and causes. The initial sacrifice of self for a lofty cause may be self-transcendent. But causes of this sort also are jealous and take us over. Our freedom does not remain. I may give myself to another, or to others. But unless the giving is reciprocal, these others will take me over, and my freedom is lost. Furthermore, if the giving is reciprocal, the selves on both sides are maintained as they are, and the giving is incomplete.

Where then is a giving that is whole and entire, and can still be maintained?

There is only one such giving—that total sacrifice of the self to the transcendent which is the central act of Christian faith. As a result of this act, the self is not taken over by any finite power. It is returned to itself for a way of existing that is no longer centered in itself but in what is wholly other, and, therefore, self-transcending. In such service there is perfect freedom. This is the heart and core of the Christian ethic.

3. *Christian Existence*

In the light of this dialectic of human freedom, let us now attempt to bring together these distinct phases of Christian ethics. We have arrived at this through a contrast with the traditional ethics of self-realization as though it were another species of the genus ethics. But now we should be able to see that we have made a leap *eis allo genos*. This is not an ethics at all, but a way of existing in the world. It does not provide us with a method of calculating the success and failure of our works, but suggests a way of interpreting our life in the world as a whole that arises from the self-revealing of our lived existence. It is concerned not so much with abstract laws and principles as with the concrete persons for the sake of whom all laws and principles are laid down. It leads us not toward self-satisfaction but toward freedom and self-transcendence. It presupposes a realization of the conditions required for personal existence.

As a way of life and thought, it must be actually followed in the concrete. In this sense, it is more than a mere possibility and calls for realization of some kind. But this is far from realization in the traditional, Aristotelian sense. This is a dialectical realization only through sacrifice. Though grounded on a getting and having, in itself it is rather a giving and becoming. Instead of works to be produced, it calls for faith to be enacted. It is guided not by a backward-looking hope but by a forward-looking historicity. Rest in the self chains existence, and divides it from itself. The free person, on the other hand, is open to self-transcendence. This freedom cannot be realized. It can only be held by a continuous self-sacrifice in history.

It may be said of this Christian philosophy, as is said of Kantian ethics, that it is purely formalistic and tells us nothing about precisely what we ought to do. This is true, because Kant also glimpsed the radical character of human freedom and saw very clearly that, being a world in itself, it could never be reduced to any object or set of objects in the world. Any attempt to fit the individual and his world into a closed system of doctrine and to prescribe therefrom what he ought to do is a violation of human freedom. Hence in the end it will only breed confusion and rebellion. This has often happened in our history, and is now too well known to be seriously repeated by thinkers who are free to examine their ultimate presuppositions.

Hence the Christian philosopher, who must be free in this sense, will abandon the idea of a closed system, and will make no attempt to prescribe to the individual what he should do in so far as he acts as a person. He will know too well that love is beyond the law and will therefore follow the example of Paul, who, in his great description of love (I Cor. 13) never tries to say just what love will do, but rather conveys a living sense of its moving spirit. Following this example, the Christian philosopher, in his interpretation of human existence, will be concerned not so much with what is to be done as how. In trying to reveal these existential structures as clearly as he can, he will constantly remember that they must be lived to be understood, that they must be rediscovered and reinterpreted by each individual, and must be filled with an infinitely variable content relevant to the situation of each new generation.

He will work out his interpretation with his eyes on the guiding image of faith. But he will not think of authentic existence as limited to a sacred region of religious history, and will not ignore secular experience and history. Such existence has been more clearly revealed in those who were conscious of their faith. But it has also been called forth in the most unexpected places, far beyond the limits of any Church, in those less clearly and fully conscious of their aims. It has been glimpsed by all those who have refused to rest in realization, and who have opened themselves to radical self-transcendence. It has touched all those who have lost their interest in getting and possessing, and have given themselves in sacrifice. It has been felt by those who, in cases of real conflict, have been actually led to put persons above the law, and have risked their lives for freedom. It has also touched those who have abandoned all calculation for merit and recognition, and have cast their bread upon the waters for anyone to have and take. This is the spirit of freedom in faith.

Having tried to convey something of this spirit as it may be manifested in the individual person, we must now turn to the human group. Is it capable of existing in this way? If not, how then does it exist? and to what norms is it subject? With these problems we shall deal in the following chapter.

Chapter Seven

THE GAP BETWEEN INDIVIDUAL
AND SOCIAL ACTION

In the last chapter we examined the Christian ethics of love and self-transcendence which is open to the individual person. It is now time for us to recognize, however, that the free individual cannot exist apart from society and its social structures. In this chapter we shall, therefore, turn to some of these social forms and to the political action by which they are maintained and sometimes transformed, with a view toward clarifying them by a brief phenomenological analysis. As we proceed, we shall become increasingly aware of a striking contrast between the Christian ethic of love and sacrifice and the ethic of self interest which guides the policies of nation states as they are acutely observed by such an analyst as Hans Morgenthau,[1] for example.

In the concluding section of this chapter, we shall turn to this gap between individual and social action and shall subject it to a more careful examination which will lead us to raise the following questions. What is the relation of the human person to the group? Has this relation been misunderstood by rationalist thought in the past? Does modern phenomenology give us any ground for a new way of understanding this relation? In the light of such an understanding, can we hope for new conceptions which may show us how

---

[1] *In Defense of the National Interest* (New York: Knopf, 1921), especially chaps. i–iv.

this gap and other cleavages we have noted, like faith versus reason, and religion versus culture, can be bridged. In our last chapter (VIII), we shall sketch out an answer to these questions. But before this, we must try to clarify our understanding of certain basic social attitudes and structures, first of all the notions of communion and community.

1. *Communion and Community*

The child is born into a community whose world is already established. This community introduces him to its world in satisfying his basic needs throughout the prolonged period of infancy. During this period, the child learns to participate with those who care for him. He develops a global view which centers as much in others as in himself. In this way he absorbs the community within himself, and for a long while he is this community. The sense of his own self that belongs to him is a later acquisition, and even then he is himself only in relation to other persons with whom he exists. But from this time on, he makes his own choices of the possibilities offered to him, and slowly works out his own way of being in the world. No matter how he chooses, he is always with others, and the different groups to which he belongs show the different values with which he has identified. There is no person apart from a community, and no community which is not constituted by persons.

The primary group is constituted by the I-Thou encounter so poignantly described by Buber. "The *Thou* meets me. But I step into direct relation with it. Hence the relation means being chosen and choosing, suffering and action in one; just as any action of the whole being, which means the suspension of all partial actions and consequently of all sensations of actions grounded only in their particular limitation, is bound to resemble suffering. The primary word *I-Thou* can be spoken only with the whole being. Concentration and fusion into the whole being can never take place through my agency, nor can it ever take place without me. I become through my relation to the *Thou;* as I become *I,* I say *Thou.*

"All real living is meeting." [2]

The Thou is not a mere object in the world, but a world that confronts and questions me. Every meeting is a challenge to growth and expansion. The child lives in this personal world, which has nothing to do with animism, but is a direct extension of his being. He does not project himself into things. He is these things as they help him or oppose him. Things come later as an abstraction. As Buber says: "Every *Thou* in the world is by its nature fated to become a thing, or continually to reenter the condition of things. In objective speech, it would be said that every thing in the world, either before or after becoming a thing, is able to appear to an *I* as its *Thou.* But objective speech snatches only at a fringe of real living. The *It* is the eternal chrysalis, the *Thou* the eternal butterfly. . . ." [3] The thing is the product of an intellectual abstraction. It can be observed there before me from a detached point of view. It is just what it is, and can be analyzed into a sum of distinct properties and qualities. The person is never just what he is but always transcends himself. He cannot be observed from the outside; he can only be encountered and understood from the inside by an active sympathy.

There are small groups founded on I-Thou relations where there is a genuine communion between the members. In such a communion the individual can participate with something like the whole of his existence, and his own inner development can be shared. Here the chasm between free existence and group structure can be bridged. But such communion is hard to maintain. It exists between the living members, and has no life of its own. The individual estab-

---

[2] M. Buber, *I and Thou* (New York: 2d ed.; Scribners, 1958), p. 11.
[3] *Ibid.,* p. 17.

lishes himself in the communion actively, and finds his own way within it according to choices of his own. Such rules as are necessary can be freely determined, and may be constantly transcended by an uncalculating sympathy and love. The members are sometimes ready to restore broken relations by acts of forgiveness, and distributive justice can be maintained by little acts of sacrifice not called for by any obligation.

This personal action is centrifugal, moving outward toward something transcending the ego and its fixed interests. The individual source of these self-giving acts is an integral person, not a social role or personage. Such communion can be found in intimate associations like the family, the friendship group, and the sect where all the members are known to one another. But it is always restricted to a small number of persons, and even here authentic manifestations are very rare. Most of the groups and institutions which now dominate our social life show a pattern that is quite different.

These groups extend far beyond anything that the individual can of himself directly know. They outlast him in time, and far outreach him in power. As institutions, they are already in a state of being established (*in statuere*). The child is thus born into them. Instead of actively finding his way, he is allotted a given position. Instead of existing solely in and between its living members, it exists in abstraction from them, and beyond them, and lives a peculiar life of its own. Since its operations extend beyond the range of any direct understanding of the individual, their primary ends must be clearly defined, and their rules and norms spelled out in objective language. Its buildings and technical implements are visible, and many of its large-scale acts can be observed and objectively reported. Hence it exists in the third person as a thing rather than in the first as a person.

I know that it is indirectly through the impersonal effects it exerts on me, as I perceive a thing only through the light that it sends to my eyes. I cannot meet it directly and let it express its inner being to me. It has no inner "subjective" being of its own but, like an orator, exists only for others in the public eye. It literally is only what it is said and seen to be. Thus it does not speak for itself but only through representatives, like the judge or the executioner. And these intermediaries also speak not for themselves as integral persons. They speak as personages, playing the role that has been allotted to them.

The institutional act is not directed toward anything transcendent beyond its province. Being instituted by an act of sharp abstraction and exclusive definition, it must remain in that objective area which is its own, and must try to master and possess the objects which belong to it. Hence its operations are centripetal, always governed by self-interest and impersonal reasons of its own, *raisons d'état*. An institution exists in the manner of a thing. It is not free but acts in accordance with rules and regulations. We cannot love it as we love a person. Nevertheless we cannot separate ourselves from such institutions and, indeed, our very existence depends upon them.

Ultimately they must be understood in the wider horizon of personal existence from which they have been abstracted. Hence we try to bestow a sort of secondary personal being upon them, and refer to them not as corporate persons (this would be going too far) but as corporate personalities. This process is aided by the fragmentary myths which gather around them, and as we shall see, some of the most important can elicit feelings of surprising poignancy and intimacy.

We have no time, of course, for an exhaustive review of social attitudes. In the next section we shall single out certain types which are now important for a brief review. The first of these is the feeling known as patriotism, which binds the individual to his people and his native soil and thus begins to link him from childhood with social institutions, like civilization and the state, which are more abstract in nature and wider in extent.

2. *Patriotism*

We seldom focus this feeling for the Fatherland as a distinctive phase of our human existence in the world. We do not clearly distinguish it from nationalism, but think of it only as an approximate synonym for that collective egotism by which one tends to identify oneself with the interests of one's nation as it is, and to exalt it over the rest. But this is a serious oversimplification which ignores certain essential differences that can be brought out by phenomenological analysis.

The finitude of human existence requires that it be rooted in a certain living space where it is at home. Without such roots, it lacks any firm ground for self-expression, and merely wanders at random in response to external pressures. The authentic feeling of patriotism is a piety toward the past which is felt by the living person himself. It includes the love that I feel toward my parents and my ancestors who prepared the way for me in the land that I know as my own. In so far as I merely regard this past objectively, I think of it as over and gone. But there is a deeper sense in which it belongs to me as the past that I am, have, and have been.

This past is never inclosed within a subjective mind. It is always projected into a living space with which I also participate. Thus the country dweller identifies himself with the familiar paths around his native village. They belong to his being. It is *his* air that he breathes, *his* water he drinks, and *his* mountains that loom on this horizon. The exile who wanders in strange countries does not feel this way. Strange perils threaten him on all sides, and he is not at home. It is not *his* air that he breathes, *his* water he drinks, or *his* people with whom he converses in *his* own tongue.

To a lesser degree, this absence of a homeland is felt today by the urbanized city dweller and the uprooted proletariat of the Western world. Assigned to servile tasks by an impersonal system hardly capable of a feeling like gratitude, these people lack any real integration into their community. Their feeling of exile and alienation was poignantly expressed in a speech to the Roman plebeians ascribed to Tiberius Gracchus by Plutarch: "The savage beasts in Italy have their particular dens, they have their places of repose and refuge; but the men who bear arms, and expose their lives for the safety of their country, enjoy in the meantime nothing more in it but the air and light; and having no houses or settlements of their own, are constrained to wander from place to place with their wives and children." According to him their commanders were guilty of a ridiculous error when "they exhorted the common soldiers to fight for the sepulchres and altars; when not any amongst so many Romans is possessed of either altar or monument, neither have they any houses of their own or hearths of their ancestors to defend. They fought, indeed, and were slain, but it was to maintain the luxury and the wealth of other men." [4] This proletarian protest goes far deeper than any purely economic readjustments, and involves the roots of our common life. This demand is for a place in the world of the living.

Hence the aim of most revolutions is to establish a new and more inclusive Fatherland. It is a mistake to think of revolutionaries as unpatriotic men. Many of them, like Rousseau and Jefferson, were deeply rooted in the life space of their countries and imbued with a deep love for their people and their native soil. But this personal love is not closed. It is open to the future and filled with hope. If this is, on the whole, a sound description of patriotism, we

[4] *Plutarch's Lives,* trans. Clough (Everyman; New York: E. P. Dutton, 1915), III, 132–133.

can see that it is very different from the nationalism with which at the present time it is so often confused.

Nationalism is a special phenomenon which results from the propaganda of mass media, whereas patriotism, as we have described it, is a universal phase of human existence which is found in all cultures, and even in an analogous form in primitive mythical societies. The former is an impersonal mass emotion which one shares with a crowd. Patriotism, on the other hand, is a personal feeling of anchorage in my native soil and history which I can feel alone. Nationalism may be directed toward certain essential human values, but it is always moved by ephemeral values which are relative to the special history of a given people at a certain time. Nationalism is a form of collective egotism which accepts its interests as they stand, and seeks to maintain them and expand them as they are by external conquest and violence. Patriotism, on the other hand, is a form of love which can be exercised only by persons. It is not blind but, like all love, it has a certain clairvoyance which makes it open to the future. It is guided by hope, and does not rest on a forceful assertion of what it is at present.

It must be granted, however, that at the present time this hope is for the most part channeled into the blind urge of collective egotism. We must now ask: Is this necessary? Can this rootedness, which is open to further growth, be directed without loss into a more essentially human and more universal horizon? Is this a mere daydream? Or is there an actual force we can all see at work in the vague complex of the nation-state which might lead it, and is perhaps now leading it, in such a universal direction? There is such a force.

3. Civilization and Culture

Man no longer directly confronts the realm of nature. He lives in a social world of roads, fields, buildings, and other artifacts which have profoundly modified the natural environment. We use the term *civilization* for all the works of man that have left a permanent mark on the environment. These works are cumulative so that the creative achievements of one age are passed on to the next. Our present civilization is, therefore, a deposit which has come down to us from all the ages of the past; and the child, in becoming civilized, must recapitulate the whole of this human history. Thus in learning to think about himself and the world, the child first goes through a mythical stage, and then a rational stage roughly corresponding to the development of our Western culture.

These works of civilization fall into many kinds and affect everything we think and do, our clothes, our houses, our means of travel, the gestures and language by which we converse. In general, they fall into two distinct kinds which are worthy of a brief comment.

In the first place, there are the various tools and implements like food, furniture, streets, and apparel which we use for living, and the productive enterprises which make them. In their various regions and meaningful connections with one another, they constitute a basic area of the life-world which we may call the civilized environment or the region of technology. The knowledge which guides us in the production and the technical use of such instruments is what we call *science*. This science and the technology it directs are now a highly developed co-operative enterprise proceeding in all parts of the world. Individual scientists carry on the work in their separate fields, but these fields are now so highly specialized and complex that no one mind can master them all. Nevertheless science itself makes use of these individual contributions, and now seems to expand and grow of itself, like a coral reef, into wider and more complex formations.

It is also important to notice that its observations, laws, and operations are universal. They are not restricted to any one time or place. The observations can be made by any detached observer, and the operations can be performed anywhere by anyone with the requisite skill and apparatus. It has given us a great power over subhuman nature. Thus in recent times it has enabled the world population to treble itself and has completely revolutionized our common way of life.

This brings us to a second branch of civilization which touches our human existence more directly. In giving us a new grasp on things, the works of civilization have also given us a new grasp on ourselves. They have enabled us to discover new values and to understand ourselves in different ways. In the primitive mythical community, the basic values of what we now call language, religion, art, philosophy, and government were all woven together into an organic unity. But with the coming of reason and history, this unity was destroyed and each branch was left free to grow in its own way, separate from the rest. As a result of this, different civilizations in different parts of the world developed these fields in different ways and ordered them into different patterns. This pattern of language and the basic human values which have been worked out in the history of a particular civilization are what we call its culture.

It differs from civilization in the following ways. Culture is concerned with human values which must be incorporated in acts performed by the individual person himself. Such acts as worship, the appreciation of beauty, and insight have an intrinsic value in themselves. Culture is, therefore, closer to the living individual than civilization. This appears both in its history and in its present mode of assimilation. Thus the history of philosophy and the history of art crystallize around individual names and individual achievements. Also they *touch* the individual more closely than technology. No child can avoid learning his mother tongue and the values it incorporates, and it is through the cultural values thus transmitted to him that he is able to find himself and order a world of his own.

These values are rooted in the particular history of a people in its living space. Nevertheless, in intention they point to something universal beyond the different nations and countries. As long as freedom still exists, they are open to further development. Being rooted in a native soil, however, they show a wide range of variation. The culture of a people cannot be understood by an impersonal observation of objects and artifacts. It can be understood only by a sympathetic rethinking and reproduction of the way of life and the human world to which they belong. We may summarize this contrast by saying that culture is much closer to the personal centers of freedom who alone give existence to civilization and enable it to grow.

4. *The Nation*

The nation is now a dominant form of social organization and in union with the state, as the nation-state, a development of modern history since the French Revolution, it is now threatening us with world destruction. The nation as such is a complex structure involving many factors. One of these is the possession of a geographic territory with fixed limits, though the history of the Jewish people should guard us against thinking of this as essential. Another is political independence, though the Polish nation survived long periods of conquest in which this was lacking. A third factor is a permanent balance between the economic interests of different groups in the national community, though many nations have survived internal revolutions.

We must now be on our guard against the concept of race, because of its biological indeterminacy and the fantastic modern myths that have been built around it. Nevertheless, it is probably true that the persistence of a certain biological type, usually of a mixed order as in Mexico, is characteristic of national histories. We should probably think of all these objective factors as being necessary conditions, no one of which is a sufficient condition for national existence.

More important than these is what we may refer to as the inner life of the nation, which brings us to the sphere of the free person.

We have noted how the concrete urges of patriotism may be led into wider and more universal channels by civilization and culture. This is theoretically possible in some instances, and to a certain degree is actually realized. But in our situation in history there is a formidable obstacle that stands between—the nation-state. We shall now break this synthetic structure into its component elements and examine them one by one.

Civilization is concerned with instrumental values which can be incorporated in subhuman things. The personal use of such things serves higher concerns, but has little intrinsic value of its own. A glance at the history of science and technology will show us that this enterprise is farther from the existing individual than his culture and his native tongue. Thus we have noted how science, while it uses the works of individuals, seems to advance and to proliferate of itself, apart from individual guidance and control. No child can now grow up without using technological instruments. But he may use them only in an instrumental manner, and if they come to be of basic concern to him, this is only by their being brought into relation with the human values of his culture.

The impersonal values of civilization are universal and are detached from any particular living space. They can be understood and utilized by any detached observer, at any time, anywhere, and show no essential variations from one nation to another. Active sympathy is unnecessary for the understanding of science and technology. In fact, it is an obstruction that must be suppressed in favor of a cool detachment that simply observes and analyzes each object as it comes. These artifacts of civilization condition and limit personal existence, but they are far from personal freedom and, indeed, they exist on another plane. So far as they enter it and determine it directly, they result only in slavery and distortion.

We have noted the person who is always present. Here we must remember that, in spite of its abstract and objective character, the nation is made up of persons, and cannot exist without them. They have contributed a certain style of existing which is visible in the scenery, clothing, speech, and attitudes of the people. This common way of life has been worked out through a long history, guided by the choices of individual leaders which continue to receive common support throughout succeeding generations. These repeated choices, constantly changing and developing through individual creative power, nevertheless leave behind them an established pattern of values expressed in the religion, art, and language of the people. Such a pattern of value, which determines the meaning of the national world, is always found in a living nation. This common style of life is essential. It is transmitted to coming generations not only by the teaching of formal schools but by that informal teaching through example and imitation which is constantly proceeding in every walk of life, and is the very life blood of the national group.

When this educational process breaks down, when the common values are no longer understood and loved, the life of the nation is threatened. Hence in order to avoid this calamity, every nation is impelled by its collective self-interest to interpret its history in grandiose mythical terms, and by a ceaseless propaganda to defend its own pattern of values as wholly righteous and even supreme. Since the history of any nation is filled with error and accident, and since its scheme of values is always relative and incomplete, this collective self-interest tends to expand as a destructive force which we now recognize as nationalism. If it cannot be contained and controlled, perhaps by the separation of the nation from the state, or by some new creative movement at a higher level, it may lead to world destruction.

5. Law and Government: The State

We are now able to distinguish the government from the nation, though we are as yet far from any real separation of the two. The nation, as we have seen, is a fusion of many factors loosely bound together in space and time. It is the sense which is emerging from the common exigencies and choices of a people thrown together and living a concrete history. Government on the other hand, l'état, the state, is a legal order, the structure of a nation's life so far as it can be codified and regulated. This legal conception grew up with the notion of a public domain taking precedence over every individual interest, and requiring certain general functions to be performed for the common good. The status and rights of every member of the community can be abstractly defined, as well as the common duties. Special rights and duties are assigned to those performing special functions. This system is administered by permanent bureaus and courts whose authority and power grow through the generations, as past decisions are accepted by custom, and as life becomes increasingly complex.

This power may be fused with that of the nation, and governed by a single individual or group, as in the totalitarian nation-state. In this case, the legal order may be distorted by national self-interest, and used to suppress all personal freedom and creativity. Hegel prepared the way for such abuses in his conception of an objective spirit which is incarnate in the national group and which takes precedence over all individual aspiration. The Fascist dictatorships have made us all familiar with the disastrous consequences of this conception when it is put into actual practice. The legal order of government becomes a mere tool for the national interest. Abandoning its real reason, which is the support of personal freedom, its structure is twisted and corrupted into a mere reason of state (*raison d'état*).

Thus the German law under Hitler became the national law of the state. Freedom of expression was stifled by a vast web of rules and regulations formulated in the national interest. Even humor and satire were suppressed.[5] Unable to choose anything for himself but death, the individual is depersonalized. The whole of his life is exhausted in the exercise of those routine functions which one performs and in the way that one performs them. Having directly experienced these corruptions at first hand in the recent past, some European thinkers now tend to dismiss the order of law and government as a vast objective system which necessarily crushes freedom and personal existence.[6] This, however, is a serious mistake.

We may see this if we consider the situation in England and the United States where the order of law and government has never been ruthlessly and consistently subordinated to the collective egotism of the nation, and has been allowed to develop with a certain degree of independence. We may feel that the actual expression of genuine freedom in these countries is not impressive. But this is not the fault of the law. It is at least clear that, when granted a certain freedom to follow its own human norms, the legal system

---

[5] An illuminating account of this will be found in Alfred Stern's interesting study, *Philosophie du rire et des pleurs* (Paris: P.U.F., 1949), III, 224–225.
[6] Cf. G. Gusdorf, *Traité de l'existence morale* (Paris: Colin, 1949), pp. 254–258.

of the state can protect the rights of the individual person against mass hysteria, and can support the expression of personal freedom when this occurs.

So far we have been concerned with the analysis of distinguishable social structures one by one. These structures, however, must be established, maintained, and sometimes transformed by a social mode of action which we distinguish sharply from individual action by the use of the term *political.*

What is politics? And how does it differ from individual behavior?

It is to these questions that we shall turn in the following section.

6. *Politics*

The first thing we must once again note concerning political action in contrast to individual existence is that it lacks subjectivity. The nation-state of course acts. But if we seek out who precisely is acting, we seek in vain. We may find a king, a president, a minister of state who is a person. But he is not acting as a person. He is acting in behalf of something else, the group. This group has no subjective being in a conscious self of its own. It exists only in self-conscious persons. How? As they objectify themselves in terms of certain common features and interests which they share. The group as such has no subjective existence of its own. It is an abstract object brought before the minds of distinct individuals. This is why Hegel called it objective spirit (*objectiver Geist*). But this is not the whole story. We must not forget the individuals who conceive this common object. Concretely speaking, the group is a number of individual persons conceiving of themselves abstractly and objectively in terms of common traits they share. This first factor (the existing individuals) is likely to be forgotten, for it transcends our powers of comprehension. I cannot understand a million individuals as existing persons, or even a hundred. I can understand them only by bringing them under a single concept, as Greeks, as Russians, or as Communists. But this is an abstraction which exists only as a project shared by separate individuals in very different ways, ranging from devotion to disagreement and rebellion. Nevertheless it does exist as a real aspect of the thought and behavior of the component members. Both factors (the concrete individuals and the abstract object) exist, and both must be borne in mind if we are to understand the life of a community. In any living community these factors must be in tension with each other, or it must decline. If the common object fades away, the community falls into chaos. If the individuals give themselves over to the group and become objectified, it falls into stagnant decline. Both factors are essential.

The component members can conceive of themselves only as a common object before their minds. Nevertheless this object is no mere figment. It is founded on shared existential traits. The individuals inhabit a common land. They may be descended from common ancestors. They share common needs, which are objectified as common ends. These ends call forth common urges and aspirations which elicit common acts. Such acts, when repeated, crystallize into customs and institutions, which gain a stable position in a public world of their own, the world of politics. This world includes regions of public action, like farming, mining, fishing, manufacture, and distribution, ordered purposefully toward each other, and ultimately toward a final end, the survival and welfare of the community. If we ask, Who is this community? no clear answer can be given, for it is no person. The question is badly put. Nevertheless, it would be wrong to conclude that it is wholly impersonal.

It is a collective object founded on shared aspects of personal existence. Hence it can be justifiably conceived as a corporate personality, and felt through personal symbols. Strictly speaking, however, it is not a person, for it lacks any subjectivity of its own. It exists, but it has no existence of its own. It exists not in and for itself (self-consciously) but only in persons, and *for them* as a common object. It has a certain purposive unity of its own and endures through time, outlasting the life of any given individual. Through its individual members it deliberates and acts historically. But because of the different objective existence from which it springs, it is important to recognize that this political action is radically distinct from the personal action of an individual. The former is necessarily governed by a concern for self-realization, while the latter, in so far as it retains its freedom and subjectivity, is not necessarily so governed. In order to emphasize this essential difference, we shall refer to our discussion of self-realization ethics in Chapter V (pp. 155–166). In this ethics we shall find the general pattern of objective political action, which is contrasted with that of personal action in the following ways.

Our personal acts arise from the depths of our being and express a way of existing in the world to which not only objective thought, but feeling and every revealing power at our disposal have made essential contributions. These insights and revelations are not restricted to clearly marked intervals of deliberation. They are maintained and modified, both deliberately and indeliberately, throughout the whole course of life. They contribute not only to social order but to a life of self-formation as well. This personal life is neither "subjective" nor "objective." It includes both factors in an overarching way of being-in-the-world. This way is not determined either with respect to its "means" or its "end." The end is open and subject to question. It may be decided by a radical choice that is no compromise but affects the quality of the world which we inhabit, and our existence as a whole.

Political action, on the other hand, arises from a process of deliberate calculation which is restricted to definite intervals of time. In such calculations an effort is made to escape from every "subjective" feeling and passion. As a result, they abstract from the personal pole of existence, and fall within an objective frame. Only those motives and interests are seriously considered which can be brought before the mind as objects and quantitatively conceived. If, in such a discussion, someone expresses a personal feeling or passion that cannot be so conceived, this is at once ruled out of order as "subjective" and inexact. In such deliberations the end is never in question. It is taken for granted as a maximum realization of the greatest number of interests already present. Hence political deliberation concerns means only and never the end. If the end itself is seriously called in question, this is revolution. The time for deliberation is over, and force must intervene. Thus in politics force takes the place of that radical choice and freedom which lie beyond the range of objectivist reflection. Prudential calculation of this kind can never result in a radical choice and a new way of being in the world. It can only result in a compromise between already existing interests in an already established world-frame.

My personal action grows not merely from detached observations of myself and others as objects but from revealing powers that inhabit it. These powers are able to take account of my whole situation in the world, or myself as I already am and hope to be, as well as of external forces and persons around me. They enable me to understand myself and others not from the outside only, but from the inside also, as we are actively engaged in the risks of our personal endeavors. Such understanding is not restricted to abstract norms and principles. It can grasp the individual in the full integrity of his being, not merely as a case, or as the example of some class. Hence it is not primarily concerned with the abstract processes of either induction or deduction, but rather with a direct grasp of existence as it shows itself to be. Hence the existing person is able to listen to the voice of his conscience which can call all his norms in question, and can lead him beyond all replaceable functions to those peculiar things which only he can do.

Political action, on the other hand, is governed by a calculation which abstracts from the subjective, and is directed exclusively toward what can be brought before the mind as an object. This mind is not located anywhere. It gazes on things from the worldless point of view of a detached observer who reports on what anyone would see from anywhere. Such reports are called "objective" and "unbiased." The concrete individual is opaque to such an ideal observing mind which can understand him only as an example of some universal principle or norm. This man is not a free person. He is a Russian, a German, a white man, or an anarchist, or a complex set of such abstract characters. This mode of objective reflection cannot understand the concrete needs of this person here and now. So it jumps to the universal needs of man in general, and the kinds of acts that must be performed if these needs are to be satisfied. These kinds of acts can be formulated as universal principles which constitute a law of nature that is valid for all men everywhere. Political reflection usually starts from abstract principles of this kind, and then passes to the concrete needs of an existing community so far as they fall under the former.

This pattern of rational reflection appeals to universal norms and principles to protect it from the voice of conscience. Instead of seeking for what I alone can do, it seeks for that which anyone would do in similar circumstances. For social action, such objective reflection is indispensable, since abstract grounds of agreement must be found. But to the open world of the free individual it does not apply, except through an endless maze of casuistry which only makes the gulf more evident.

The individual person is not chained to a fixed, formal pattern which excludes all other alternatives and is to be either realized or unsatisfied. He is free and open to self-transcendence. His final end is not fixed by nature but open to radical choice. His acts are not accidents of a substantial self which remains unaltered. He *is* these acts, and through them he either becomes or loses himself. But he cannot really become himself without giving up the self that he was before. Genuine becoming always requires genuine sacrifice. It is not so much a self-realizing through possessing as a history of becoming through giving, in which there is no sharp distinction of means and ends. This history of becoming-through-giving is ever unfinished. So it is certainly not an end. Nevertheless there is a value in the very living of it. So it cannot be dismissed as a mere means.

In order to establish a civilized community, however, different individuals must agree on certain ends to be achieved, and on a certain fixed pattern of procedure. This basic agreement as to what they are objectively, and what their ends are to be, is formulated whether in a written constitution or embodied in a continuous tradition. All social deliberation moves within this fixed framework, and governs political acts by which the objective pattern is either realized in part or frustrated. Hence as we have pointed out, every social ethics is an ethics of realization. In this form of action, there is a sharp distinction between means and end. By instrumental action having no objective value, ends may be realized in which the group may rest. As we have pointed out, social ethics follows this pattern of self-realization, and moral theory in the West has constantly attempted to assimilate personal action to this pattern. But as we have suggested, this is a serious mistake. Instead of a realizing through possessing, personal action is a becoming through giving.

Such free action must be ultimately moved by a faith in something transcending it. Otherwise the person will become enslaved to what he is, and lose his freedom. This action cannot take the form of works which the agent can observe and judge, and from which he can stand aside. It must rather take the form of acts into which he throws the whole weight of his being, and for which he takes a final risk.[7] Finally, for these acts, no matter what they may be, he can take no credit. In the first place, they are never finished. Every life is incomplete. And in the second place, he has no access to a norm beyond his being and his world with which he can compare himself, and through which he can then take credit, for all his norms are in his world.

Political action, on the other hand, must be grounded in a common agreement of many individuals concerning a possible common end for the realization of which there is ground for hope. Such an end is therefore not transcendent. It is only a realization of what they already are. But the person himself is free, and open to what is radically other. In this way and in others, his world is richer, and not enclosed in any objective frame. Hence he can stand aside from the social works and functions he performs as a member of the body politic. He is not these works. He causes them, and *does* them with a certain objective part of himself from which he remains distinct. Hence when they meet the accepted social standard of realization, he may take credit for them, or when they are deficient, he must take the blame. But when the individual takes his life in his hands, and acts as a free person, he acts with the whole of himself and his

---

[7] William James clearly recognized this and other distinctive features of personal action. See *The Will to Believe and Other Essays*, pp. 91–97 and also "Great Men and Their Environment," *ibid.*, pp. 216 ff.

world. He cannot observe himself from any external posision, and compare himself with an objective norm. He and his world and his norms are all at stake together. This is not a *work* but an *act* of faith, unfinished. Hence he should not take credit or boast of such an act, whatever it may be.

Such personal action is clearly aware of the historic past, which weighs it down and limits its possibilities. It is precisely this past which is risked in a project for the future. Such free existence is, therefore, rightly characterized as a forward-looking historicity. The past that I am is given up and sacrificed for the sake of a new, creative future. My bread is cast upon the waters, and offered up to another self, transcending what I am. This is the only way in which freedom can be maintained.

Political calculation, on the other hand, is based upon a priority of the past. Its aim is to realize a nature that has already been agreed upon in the form of an accepted constitution. This realization, of course, is uncertain. History may frustrate the community. But its objective nature is clearly defined and fixed. As George Mead clearly saw, it was only through the personal orientation of Christianity that the idea of progress was first cultivated and brought to fruition in purposive social change in modern times.[8] In the nineteenth century political constitutions capable of revising themselves were finally established. Such revisions, however, though they originally come from individual initiative, must not break a historic continuity with the past. They are based not so much on a forward-looking historicity as on a backward-looking hope. That is, we hope not so much for a new future related only dialectically to the past as for a continued development and realization of what has been already achieved. In this kind of history, the

[8] Cf. *Mind Self and Society* (Chicago: University of Chicago Press, 1955), pp. 293–294.

results of freedom may be maintained, but freedom itself fades away. A past self is preserved and realized. It is not transcended in freedom.

We now have a contrast before us. Personal action is open to a radical choice of ends as well as means. It is concerned with the individual in his concrete integrity. It is a dialectical becoming which involves the sacrifice of a past self, as well as the coming of a new self to be born, and is centered in something transcendent rather than in a structure already formed. It expresses itself in *acts* where the self is totally present rather than in *works* from which the self can stand aside, and is guided by a forward-looking historicity. Political action, on the other hand, follows a calculation of means exclusively, not ends. It is centered in a fixed constitution already understood and objectified, and is governed by abstract principles and laws. It issues in works that can be objectified and compared with extrinsic norms, and is governed by a backward-looking hope.

If political history can be truly characterized in this way, it is not surprising that, as we have observed (Chapter VI), an insurmountable chasm seems to yawn between social and individual ethics. It is to this chasm that we must now again direct our attention.

7. The Gap

The Christian ethics of love and sacrifice is poignantly expressed in the Sermon on the Mount. Love your enemies; be perfect like the sun which sheds its light on the good as well as on the evil; be not anxious for your life. This ethics is still alive in the hearts of Western individuals, and is still used as a standard for judging the significance of individual conduct.

But when we turn to the human group, and particularly

to the dominant group of our time, the nation-state, this ethics of love and compassion becomes fantastic. Aside from small religious groups of the sectarian type, and here only in rare instances, no large political organization, such as an empire or a state, has ever voluntarily sacrificed itself for its enemies. Indeed we do not even seriously use this standard in judging the behavior of nation-states, for we take it for granted that any nation which acted in this way would be at once gobbled up in the struggle for power, which is the essence of politics. A group which failed, like the sun, to distinguish between good and evil from its point of view would not only cease to be political but would cease to be at all, thus abandoning all the real values it protects. And there can be no question that it does protect certain real values for its own citizens. Hence a group which was not anxious for its life would fail in its essential duty, and would seem to be absurd.

Thus a chasm has opened up between the religious ethics of love and compassion, and the behavior of nations with their seemingly inevitable urge to power and their *raisons d'état*. In the last section we have suggested certain basic reasons for this tragic divorce. Now we must note four more special reasons connected with our recent history.

1. For a long time in our history the structure of social life was not sharply distinguished from nature and was accepted as part of a great cosmic order over which man could exercise no free control. It was not until the time of the French Revolution that men became conscious of their social life as a human world for which they were themselves responsible.

2. But though this modern discovery has brought forth a vast literature and many attempts to change social disorder, this order, as it is called, has proved itself to be extremely resistant to moral or even rational change. So far, it has seemed to live a strange life of its own (described by Hegel) almost wholly indifferent to moral and religious ideals (see the preceding section, six).

3. The only means, so far, of directing group policy seems to be a crude mass propaganda which appeals only to group egotism and national interest.

4. Finally, this debasement of social existence seems to be only one example of a general phenomenon that is evident in all social life. Group structures are first established by the creative thought and action of gifted individuals, which radiate out to large numbers of followers and descendants. But as it moves from its source, this radiation loses its clarity and intensity. The ideas become oversimplified and shallow, and the institutionalized habits which follow from them become rigid and inflexible. This law of institutional decline seems to apply to every region of social life, including the religious.

The reasons we have now suggested are perhaps sufficient to account for the striking fact, noted by many thinkers like Reinhold Niebuhr [9] and Berdyaev,[10] that we now employ a dual standard of ethics, one to the individual and another, quite different, to the state. Thus the ruthless assertion of force, lying, murder, and even mass destruction which would be regarded as crimes, if committed by any individual, are accepted as normal and even praiseworthy, if committed for reasons of state. Individual ethics often emphasizes such values as love, compassion, and sacrifice which are open to a religious interpretation. Social "ethics," on the other hand, is closed to such values, recognizing at best only the values of national interest. It is far below the level of any pure, religious morality, and seems so debased that it is a question as to whether it is an ethics at all, or only a forced response to external pressures.

[9] Cf. *Moral Man and Immoral Society* (New York: Scribners, 1932).
[10] *Slavery and Freedom* (New York: Scribners, 1944).

In the West, there have been three ways of understanding this strange divorce from a religious point of view. No one of these, I think, is acceptable to sound religious thought anywhere in the world at the present time.

First, we may simply deny that it exists, which means pretending that some national agency, usually our own, is using its power in a way that will foster religious interests, and is, therefore, engaged in fighting a holy war either cold or hot. This view has been accepted by many groups throughout the course of Western history and is still very much alive at the present time. However, it falls before two basic criticisms. It confuses the divine mystery with a finite urge to power that is not even morally defensible. In the second place, this conception of a holy war, to be carried on by secular means, is clearly condemned in the New Testament.[11] For these reasons it deserves no further discussion.

Second, we may accept this divorce of religion from politics as simply a phase of the general distinction between the secular and the divine, which has deeply influenced Western thought since the Middle Ages. The trouble with this idea is that it, too, limits the holy by putting it in a special holy place or institution, and in its own way reduces the divine transcendence. If there is a God, He cannot be adequately conceived as merely transcending certain regions of life. He transcends the world in its entirety, and is relevant to every sphere of human existence, the secular, as it is called, as well as the holy. So I do not believe that this view can now be accepted.

There is a third position which neither accepts this terrible dichotomy as the last word of religion, nor denies it as a present fact.[12] Real politics of the nation-state is a naked struggle for power in the name of the so-called national in-

---

[11] Cf. O. Cullman, *Dieu et César* (Neuchâtel: Delachaux et Niestlé, 1956).
[12] Cf. R. Niebuhr, *Christian Realism and Political Problems* (New York: Scribners, 1953), especially chaps. vii–viii.

terest. Any attempt to justify this power politics in terms of a superior ethics, even more in terms of religion, is a mere rationalization and therefore doomed to failure. This does not mean, however, that the religious ethic of love and sacrifice is denied. It cannot be applied to the conduct of nation-states. This is simply absurd. But it can guide individual action, and can be used in a negative way as a standard to reveal the necessarily sinful character of all group action and to condemn any sentimental rationalization of this debased condition.

In the sinful situations of human history, the Christian must accept this play of power. He cannot do otherwise, for he is caught in this web of evil. So he must defend the national interest of his group in the normal way, fighting evil with evil, and force with force. As a Christian, however, he will not attempt to justify this opportunism. He is no better than his enemies, but also no worse. His religion cannot guide him here toward any practical goal. It can only tell him that every side is wrong, and that he is caught in a necessary network of evil, for which he himself, and every other man, are to some degree responsible. Like the medieval defender of the two spheres, he accepts the divorce of the sacred from the secular, but with a bad conscience, we may say.

This view has been ably defended by Reinhold Niebuhr [13] and others. It is certainly less inadequate than the other positions we have considered, and may perhaps be regarded as an unstable movement of passage toward a more coherent, religious view. As it stands, however, I do not think that it can be accepted for at least two reasons.

In the first place, while it tries to bridge the chasm between the holy and the secular, and admits a relevance of the former to the latter, this relevance is only negative, and the bridge remains an unfinished and suspended indication.

[13] *Christianity and Power Politics* (New York: Scribners, 1940); and *An Interpretation of Christian Ethics* (New York: Harper, 1935).

The secular lies in necessary isolation, and remains untouched by the creative spirit of the divine. But this is incompatible with the divine transcendence.

In the second place, from a Christian perspective, this divine spirit is essentially radiant and creative, never locked up in a detached attitude of pure negation and criticism. This is irreconcilable with the Christian notion of love, which inspires all that it touches with creative fire, and makes all things new. This view is a dialectic engaged in overcoming itself. It points in the right direction. But as it stands, it is imperfect and inadequate. To what sort of thought then may we turn?

Is there an intermediate ethics which, on the one hand, is really connected with religious devotion and sacrifice and yet, on the other, is supported by real sanctions which apply to the state? It is the failure to find such an intermediate ethics which renders the views we have been considering unstable and ineffective. Is there any such ethics? Has any germinal knowledge of it been achieved? If so, where is such knowledge to be found?

In the West an affirmative answer to these questions has been given by the tradition of natural law.[14] Its defenders claim that this objective law is based upon a common nature shared by all men, and that it can be known by the unaided human intelligence. They also claim that it is based upon the rational plan of God in the act of creation. Hence it is both divine and human, and capable of mediating between the pure ethics of love and the natural impulses of man. But this Western conception of natural law is subject to certain basic criticisms. The most important of these are the following three.

1. On the human side, its conception of a fixed and immutable human nature which can be realized only in cer-

[14] For an account of the history and meaning of natural law philosophy in the West, see Wild, *Plato's Modern Enemies and the Theory of Natural Law* (Chicago: University of Chicago Press, 1952).

tain definite ways does not do justice to human freedom and the vast variety of cultural forms it has brought forth.

2. The claim is made that natural law is closely connected with the pure religious ethics of love and sacrifice. But when carefully examined, this claim is subject to serious question both theologically and morally. It can be presumably known by any man in the natural state, apart from any distinctively religious faith or understanding. But then, as we should expect, the ethics of self-realization, or *eudaimonism,* turns out to be purely humanistic, and lacking in any real religious relevance. This ethics has much in common with utilitarianism, and it is no wonder that it has been unable to develop any cogent condemnation of power politics and the egotistic practices of the modern nation-state.

3. The religious person is inspired by the mystery of the transcendent. He is ready to give himself for the love of God and the love of his fellow men. Rare individuals here and there in all great cultures have, to some degree, approximated this idea. But we cannot expect saintly conduct from the nation-state. We need an intermediate ethics at a lower level, but directly connected with the life of love and sacrifice. Let us then ask what way of existing is most directly presupposed by such a life? The answer of the Western tradition has been law and order. Thus St. Augustine argued for the *Pax Romana* as a prerequisite for the Christian life, and placed peace, as ordered harmony, at the very center of his social theory.[15]

This persistent tendency to rank order above the values of personal existence and freedom has been another (third) error of natural law philosophy, leading to an increasing isolation of religion from politics and actual life. If religion is directly dependent on social order with no intermediary, and if peace and order can be produced by power, then the ruthless use of political power can be given at least a partial re-

[15] *De Civitate Dei* xix. chaps. 12–13.

ligious justification. But such an order cannot be produced by power alone. Hence this argument is fallacious. As we know from recent experience, there are forms of peace which stifle freedom, and the possibility of religious existence. Peace and order do not guarantee free existence. This whole value structure has been misread.

The classical distinction between nature and Grace is oversimplified and fails to focus the intermediate world of human freedom which lies between, or rather brings these two together in the sweeping horizon of the world of man. It was this failure which prepared the way for that fatal separation of religion from life which, as we have seen, is a characteristic feature of modern thought. The biological and social phases of human existence are still merged with nature, and regarded either as an objective network of causal determinations, or if partially humanized, as a network of necessary sin for which we are responsible. The religious devotion of rare individuals is something totally separate and apart. One cannot interpenetrate with the other.

But this is evidently false.

The saint, like Augustine, comes out of the world of men and continues to dwell in this world in his own peculiar way. Furthermore his acts are received by this world, and affect it in many ways. The twofold scheme is inadequate. A third term has been omitted that is covered neither by nature nor by Grace.

Religion can be aided, obstructed, and even eliminated, but it cannot be produced by external force. It requires a field of possibility, but in addition to this, the spontaneous exercise of personal choice and devotion. Without this, it is a spurious imitation. Hence we cannot argue that religion requires only peace and order that may be produced by force. This is an oversimplification. We must say rather that authentic religion first requires a free decision that rests, in turn, on a flexible order of a certain kind, which force alone can never produce. The tradition of natural law in the West has objectified this order and split it into a human part, called nature, and a divine part, called Grace. Political forces working of themselves, according to nature, will produce a natural peace on which the order of Grace is founded. Human freedom is divided between the two, and consists in being absorbed by one order or the other, or by both together.

The fact that the two orders harmonize (Grace perfects nature) is guaranteed by the unity of God, the common creator. This view, however, has broken down in the light of our historical experience. It is true that political forces working of themselves, in accordance with national interest, if they avoid total destruction, do come to rest in a kind of peace, but not one that is necessarily favorable to freedom or even humanity. Grace does not directly perfect nature. It does not work without freedom, externally and automatically. If it is to work at all in human history, Grace must first be received into the heart of man and exercised by free decision. This freedom does not consist in the mere acceptance of a given order. It acts creatively in the constitution not of a single region or sphere, but of the human world in its entirety.

As such, it is open to what is called Grace. It is through this fragile channel of personal freedom that Grace first enters human history. Hence from a religious point of view, the order of a human society must be judged on the basis of its capacity to support human freedom and personal existence on the basis of its openness to transcendence. If this is true, the person and his world can no longer be understood as included within nature, nor as included within the human group. Personal existence is a distinct level of being which cannot be reduced to other levels, but must be understood in terms of its own distinctive structures and categories. Some of these have now been clearly revealed.

In the light of these facts, how then are we to understand the exercise of free existence? In particular, if the individual is not related to the group as part to whole, how are we to understand this relation? We are here confronting a basic question of political theory to which we shall turn in the next chapter.

Chapter Eight

BRIDGING THE GAP

We have now considered the action of the individual person and the Christian patterns of self-transcendence and sacrifice to which it is open (Chapter VI and Chapter VII, section 6). We have also considered certain social structures and the political action which sustains and sometimes changes them (Chapter VII). As a result of these observations, we have indicated the gap which yawns between these two modes of action and between the moral ideals by which we judge the two (Chapter VII, section 7). It is now time for us, in this concluding chapter, to ask ourselves whether traditional moral theory offers us any hope of bridging the gap, and if not, whether this is due to certain errors or omissions that have been made. Can such errors be revealed and corrected?

These questions are certainly of interest to a Christian philosopher. We shall now attempt to approach them by first considering the relation of the person to the group (1), and then (2), certain omissions that have been made by traditional social theory in the West. After this we shall approach the question of bridging the gap from a somewhat different point of view revised by certain results of modern phenomenology (3). Finally (4) we shall conclude with a brief consideration of living problems of our time.

1. *The Person and the Group*

If we look at group patterns from the standpoint of personal freedom, several points become clear. First of all, the traditional notion of the individual as a part of the group is inadequate. In order to do justice to the facts we have uncovered, we must replace this static, objective conception by a dynamic one which is able to take account of those subjective factors which play an important role in both social and individual existence. The child is born into a social world that is already organized and established. But this world is not a static structure. It is constantly being reinterpreted and transformed. All through his life the child is meeting novel situations in new ways. Every encounter is a challenge. Every conversation is a struggle to find ways of expressing new meanings in old traditional forms.[1] In so far as he makes real choices, the individual is constantly organizing and reorganizing a world of his own. Even the least creative individual leaves behind him influences and memories which contribute something to the history of his people.

From the social and objective point of view, it is the group which precedes the individual and moulds him by its pre-existent forms. From a more dynamic and historical point of view, however, it is the creative person who runs ahead of the group with new ideas that are then assimilated into institutional structures that always lag behind. No doubt there is truth in each of these perspectives. But at any given time, there is not just one uniform, social world, including individuals. There are rather many divergent personal worlds, all sharing in a common but moving foundation. Both factors must be recognized, the common, established core with in-

---

[1] Cf. M. Merleau-Ponty, *op. cit.*, pp. 203–235.

dividual projects shooting out from it in different directions, each pulling the base from which it came in its own way, like a confused jet plane propelled by different, angular explosions.

This, of course, is only a crude metaphor. But it may serve to suggest the relational interdependence of the individual and the group, and the way in which they exist in and for each other. What we have been calling the social or public world is not a complete world at all. It is only an objective region in the worlds of existing persons. Hence it does not exist in itself and for itself, but only for others who reveal it and complete it. The individual, on the other hand, can be brought to himself only through the aid of others. But once in being, he exists in a world of his own, and in the way he chooses. In this sense, we can say that the person is in himself and for himself. But as soon as his acts are crystallized, they are manifest and exist for others in the common pool we refer to as *the public world*. But once again we must note that this is not at all a complete world but only an abstraction which exists, so far as it exists at all, in the actual world of a person. It is the person alone who not only exists objectively for others, but also in and for himself in a concrete world of his own, ordered toward his ultimate concern.

We must now notice that with the exception of the primary I-Thou group, all the social patterns we have been considering—technology, patriotism, the order of law and government, and culture—are imperfect and potential. They have no being in themselves but exist only for the free person. Hence their ultimate meaning must be understood in terms of the role they play in this personal existence. Thus technology supplies him with the means of life. His love for his land and people give him roots in his living space. Law and government protect him from violence and give him an opportunity for finding himself. Culture gives him his mother on use for himself, as we say, this self is distinct from the one working now. He is working for himself only as an other. Like an actor playing a role on the stage, his acts are in no sense self-contained but incomplete and referential. His whole attention must be focused not on how he appears to himself, but on how he appears to himself as an other. Without these others, his performance is a meaningless fragment torn from its context. It can be completed and given meaning only by other persons who exist *in* themselves and can understand and appreciate the performance *for* themselves.

In so far as he belongs to a functioning group, the individual also understands himself as an object observed by a generalized other. Thus the worker must envisage himself from the point of view of the foreman, the professor from the point of view of the generalized student, the actor from that of the audience in general, and the scientist from that of any qualified observer—what will he see and how will he judge the experiment? This kind of reflection where everything, even the person himself, is viewed from the outside as an object, is now called rational, and presses its claim to be the only legitimate mode of thought. It is radically opposed to another mode of which we are now only beginning to be aware. In this, the living individual tries to orient himself in the world by thinking not for another but for himself.

Rationalism in the past has dismissed this style of thought as eccentric and "subjective." By the use of this confused epithet, it grants that existence lies beyond its scope, but squeezes it, as a private and insignificant phenomenon, into small interstices in its vast universe of objects. As a matter of fact, it is this realm of objects which, like the actor's performance, is essentially relative and incomplete. It is clearly relative to something which understands them and also itself. If this revealing of objects is not completed by

tongue and, through this, conveys to him the human
that have been revealed in the history of his civili

But these are abstract perspectives. It is only
primary group that he meets another free person with
world other than his own which can communicat
speak for itself, unhindered by any objective frame.
encounters can, of course, occur through all these
frames. But it is only in such total encounters that the p
together with his world as a whole, comes into play.
only here that he meets his other with whom he can
communicate, and express that free existence-in-the-
which cannot be found in any objective, social perspe
This unique level of existing has been glimpsed by a
philosophers of the Western tradition, especially by l
but usually obscured and distorted by rationalistic assu
tions. Recent phenomenology has at last succeeded in b
ing it into the light.[2]

So now let us try to bring out as clearly as possible
main points of difference which distinguish the level
personal existence from that of group life. We are conti
ing not only two modes of being but two modes of thinki
for it is now quite clear that every kind of thought is a
of being in the world which belongs to the human pers
What we are distinguishing, therefore, are two modes
personal existence: (1) the way he lives and thinks as
longing to an objective group in the present stage of c
history, and (2) the way he lives and thinks as a free
dividual.

In so far as he belongs to a group, the individual fun
tions and thinks not for himself but for others. Thus tl
worker on the assembly line and the professor in a schoo
so far as he is a professor, are working for others. Even thoug
the worker may be putting together a car that he will late

[2] See especially, M. Merleau-Ponty, *op. cit.;* and *Existence,* ed. Rollo Ma
(New York: Basic Books, 1958).

a revealing that can manifest itself for itself, it remains a meaningless fragment torn from its context.

The objects of the human and subhuman environment are shared by a social attitude that is also shared. We think of them together as the great public world of reality into which the individual is born and which moulds him and conditions him as long as he lives. It also includes his little, private world as a peculiar subjective object within its broad confines.[3] Thus it precedes him, conditions him, and includes him. These basic theses of our traditional rationalism are still defended by the positivism and naturalism of our time. But this public world does not exist in and for itself, as is recognized when we say that it must be *shared*. As soon as we ask, Shared by whom? the objective clarity dissolves, and must be replaced, if at all, by another kind of clarity. The public world is shared by historic persons who are not shared in this way and whose worlds are prior to it. Without their creative explorations and discoveries, it could not be. The objective world, as we know it now, is what they have left behind. In this sense, they have conditioned it. Furthermore, it does not exist in itself, but only as a special perspective for the individual who is also aware of his lived existence and its many non-objective phases. Hence the shared world is in a larger frame. It is only an aspect of a personal world-horizon which is actually much broader. In the last analysis it is this world of the existing person that is prior, more basic, and more inclusive.

Let us now turn to certain temporal characteristics. The person dwells in a world of freedom which is dynamic and creative, showing marked variations from person to person and culture to culture. It can move very quickly in unpredictable ways that follow no known laws. The common

---

[3] Both Russell and Broad have used the phrases *public world* and *private world* in this way.

world of society, on the other hand, is relatively fixed and static. It moves. But it moves very slowly, like a sluggish, crawling animal, and usually in regular ways that may be predicted according to established uniformities. In this sense, it is closer to the region of nature than to the erratic world of a free person. Kant saw this difference very clearly and called this world of freedom "noumenal," or unknowable. It is true that it cannot be known by the objective methods of reason and science. When such an attempt is made, it is reduced to a set of objects and loses its freedom. In this respect Kant was right. The categories that apply to nature do not apply here. It is constituted by meanings rather than by causal laws. It cannot be analyzed into non-relational elements, nor can it be explained. Nevertheless, we should not follow Kant in calling it "noumenal." Modern phenomenology has shown that, while it cannot be explained, it can be understood by a disciplined, revealing sympathy.

Not only is its existential structure quite different from the categories that apply to objects; its very space and time are different.[4] Its life space is oriented around the human body as its center, and it is divided into places and regions of care. These characteristics distinguish it radically from any geometric or purely physical space. Personal time is also different.

As social beings, we think of time as a succession of nows. Only the present moment is real. The future is a not-yet-now; the past a now-no-longer. Time moves, like a stream, out of the past, then to the present, and finally afterward into the future. We measure this time by regular motions, like those of the hands of a watch. This is the clock-time of our everyday, social life.

The lived time of the existing person is richer, and is ordered in a different way. The future which always stretches ahead of me is not a nothing-now. It has a projective being of

---

[4] Cf. M. Heidegger, *Sein und Zeit*, so far the most penetrating study of the human *Lebenswelt*.

its own which alters as I act. It also has a being of its own which is not merely increased, but transformed as my life develops. This development is not restricted to the present, but affects all the ecstasies of my temporal existence, past and future as well as the present. It seems to originate in the future which comes to envelop the present and the past. Thus I speak of my future as ahead of me, and of my past as left behind. This time proceeds not regularly but in fits and starts, sometimes rapidly in times of decisive action, sometimes slowly in those of dull routine. It is measured not by clocks but by effort and care. This is not a time that I gaze at, but a time that I really am. It is true that I can regard myself as an object, and fit the changes of this object into the dates of calendar time. But when I do this, much has been omitted. This clock-time is derived from a temporality that constitutes my personal being, and is richer and more primordial.

In the light of this comparison, we must make a radical distinction between the world of the individual person and that of the group. It is certainly incorrect to think of society as a *whole* of which the person is a *part*. If anything, as we have indicated, it is the opposite which is true. But the categories of whole and part do not do justice to this peculiarly dynamic and intimate relation. We must recognize not merely that the person and the group have different traits and properties, but that they exist in different ways.

Social existence is not in and for itself, but incomplete and for another. Social thought is similarly incomplete and relative. It understands all things, including itself, not as they are for themselves but rather as objects, or as they appear to another. Personal existence, on the other hand, is both in and for itself. As persons we try to understand ourselves and others not as objects before another mind, but as we are in ourselves. The objects of rational, social thought constitute a special perspective which is shared by personal worlds which are in a certain sense prior and more inclusive.

Personal existence is dynamic and extremely variable, social life more sluggish and fixed. The life space of the individual is oriented by the directions of left and right and up and down which are absent from geometric, objective space. Lived time involves an integration of the three ecstasies of time, and a priority of the future which are not found in the clock-time of our social life.

Each of these modes of being is very real. Indeed, as we have noted, neither can exist without the other. There is no human individual who does not belong to groups, and there is no group that is not shared by different persons. And yet these two levels of existence are radically distinct. This is, in fact, the reason for the gap between individual and social life we have noted, and the two standards of ethics we apply to them. This is no mere accident of history, but a distinction deeply grounded in human being—the structure of our human life and consciousness. We are interested in how this gap is to be bridged. But we must first consider the way in which rationalistic thought has failed to bridge it, and even to take account of it at all.

2. Rationalistic Reduction and Failure

In the preceding pages (Chapter II) we have shown how reason and personal existence emerged together with the breakdown of primitive mythical life. But we have also noted different ways in which rational thought, now associated with the life of the human group, has failed to grasp the distinctive character of personal existence (Chapters V and VI). By way of summary we may now point out how such traditional philosophies, still influential in our own time, as Thomism, naturalism, positivism, scientism, and Marxism all agree not only in adopting an objective point of view but in subordinating the individual to the group.

For all of them, human existence as it is lived from within is discounted as something subjective and allotted an indeterminate but definitely minor place in the great objective universe. All of them regard the individual as part of the group which is prior and more inclusive. All agree with Aristotle [5] that social value takes precedence over individual value. According to St. Thomas, the individual is a part of the group,[6] and the common good is more inclusive than the particular good; according to utilitarianism the supreme value is the greatest good of the greatest number; and for Hegel and his followers, the objective spirit, which objectifies itself in the human group, takes precedence over the subjective spirit of the individual. Freedom is allowed no world of its own, but is squeezed into the interstices of natural and social structure. For Thomism, we realize our freedom only by following the natural law, and for Hegel only by following the dialectic of world history.

No one of these systems makes any sharp distinction between individual and social ethics. The same moral law applies equally and in the same way to the individual person and the group. All agree with Plato that the community is simply the individual writ large,[7] and that the individual is simply the community writ small. There is only a difference of magnitude, no qualitative distinction. For both, the end is to be found in a process of realization, governed in both cases by the same system of virtues, and the same prudential calculation. With many minor variations, one finds this same pattern running through the whole history of Western moral thought as a dominant theme.

Nevertheless, in spite of the monolithic implications of this theory, the yawning gap between individual and social behavior stares us in the face. It is evident for all to see. The

[5] *Nichomachean Ethics* i.2.
[6] *Summa Theologiae, Treatise on Law*, qu. 90. art. 2; and qu. 96. art. 4.
[7] *Republic* ii. p. 368.

theory has ignored the life-world of the human person, and the differences we have indicated. It is now refuted by well-known facts. But it has also failed in other respects. If it were true, we should expect one great system of objective reason to have developed in our Western history. This system should have acted as a unifying force, providing timeless rules and norms for the guidance of both social and individual conduct.

It is hard to reconcile this grandiose conception with other well-known facts.

The simple system of reason has disintegrated into many systems, each incorporating itself in an empire or nation state with its own kind of *raison d'état*. This is enough to show that something important has been omitted. Why should reason divide itself? Yet it has divided even more strikingly into the divergent worlds of individual thinkers, as the history of philosophy makes abundantly clear. This history may be guided by the spirit of human freedom. It is certainly not the story of the formulation of a single perennial philosophy. Underneath all these splits is the basic split between the group and the individual, which is more than a split. It is a frustrating opposition which has plagued our history from its first beginnings. On the one side, we find those defending social unity, and what they call order, for objective reasons of state. These reasons, if they were to proceed unchecked, would lead us, as we know from sad experience, to the totalitarian state. In the form of an unchecked scientism, they would lead us to the night world of 1984.

But on the other hand, we find those defending individual rights and what they call freedom. It may be that we can glimpse indications among them of a higher kind of ethics. But judging from our history, their chaos of personal reasons would lead us to the abandonment of truth in an anarchy of relativism. It is no wonder that social thought has struggled to avoid this catastrophe by attempting to work out an all inclusive system of objective reason valid for all.

But this attempt has failed.

The gap between the objective life of the group and the free human person still remains. Once again let us ask: how is this gap to be bridged? Let us now suggest an answer to this question.

3. *The Bridging of the Gap*

This will require a change in the moral understanding of ourselves as well as in our way of life. We must here use verbal symbols. But these must be existentially interpreted if they are to be understood. In the first place, we must gain a new understanding of the natural law. Our tradition is right in defending the idea that there is a moral law with real sanctions, grounded in the nature of things which applies to group behavior. A community which does not care for the education of its children is punished by ignorance and lethargy. The most adequate summary of these basic social needs in the present state of our knowledge is to be found in the *United Nations Declaration of Human Rights*. These rights and duties are well founded, and no society can ignore them without peril.

But the tradition has been wrong in maintaining that the end of social justice is a reign of peace and order in which freedom has only an abstract right to express itself. This is a serious misconception which has confused political theory throughout the centuries. The aim of social justice is not the abstract possibility of personal freedom but the actual practice of it. Therefore we must learn to judge every human institution not merely by the degree to which it fits into a system of peace and order, but by the degree to which it is open to the actual practice of freedom, something very different. It is exercised not *in* any reign of social justice, but in a world of its own, with norms and structures of a very different kind.

The natural law of social justice conditions and limits the exercise of personal freedom. It lays down positive prescriptions which may guide the affirmative actions of institutions. It tells them not only what they should not, but what they should do. It cannot legislate in this affirmative way for the living person. It reveals the necessary conditions without which he cannot exist. It shows the limits of this finite existence, and tells him what he should not do, if he is to exist at all. Such commands, however, are negative. They are entirely unable to give affirmative guidance in the exercise of personal freedom. In fact, if they are taken seriously as a systematic code of personal ethics in the classical sense, they can hamper and even destroy it. What then can be done to avoid such moral destruction? How can social institutions further the authentic exercise of personal existence? Such questions are very relevant to the critical situation of our time.

The constitutional rights of the individual must, of course, be maintained. Those of free association and expression are particularly important. But they guarantee only the possibility of freedom; they do not actively foster its exercise. For this, much more is needed. No institution is so rigid and formalized as to rule out individual expression of every kind. But much more can be done to open up traditional social patterns for personal communication and for the development of those primary groups in which the individual can think and act for himself. The cult of first names and a familiar manner at least shows a vague recognition of this need. But for the most part, this has sunk to the level of a formal convention which tends to stifle, rather than to elicit any active personal response. Indeed, the word *personal* is often used as a term of reproach, as when we ask, Why be so personal about this matter? or Why take it so personally?

Free existence cannot be maneuvered and manipulated.

The way for it can be prepared, however, by a far deeper understanding of its nature than is now conveyed by our formalized, rationalistic system of education. Here the contributions of art, literature, and music are essential.[8] As a matter of fact, it is through the revealing power of these arts that most of us learn whatever we come to know about the life-world of the living person. We can learn something about our own possibilities through a sympathetic study of history, but not if it is taught as a survey of past statistics and accomplished facts. Something about the process of world formation, and the vast range of its possibilities can be learned from a study of the history of philosophy, but only if the student is led to sense the spirit of freedom which underlies this history, and is encouraged to make experiments of his own. Our system of education has fallen into a set of rigidly separated departments which need to be broken down and cross-fertilized. A noteworthy achievement of this kind has been the new light shed on personal development by the co-operation of social psychologists, psychological sociologists, and phenomenologists in the study of what is called *basic personality*.[9]

Such programs should be encouraged, especially in the human sciences, for the task of shedding light on the personal life-world is one of crucial importance to which all the social sciences, as well as philosophy, can make essential contributions. In this field explanatory theories should give way to phenomenological insight. To explain the free human person in the concrete exercise of his conditioned freedom is to explain him away. We must approach him, wher-

---

[8] For a most suggestive account of modern art as revealing the critical situation of our time, see W. Barrett, *Irrational Man* (New York: Doubleday Anchor, 1958), chap. i, sec. 3; and chap. ii.

[9] R. Linton, *The Cultural Background of Personality* (New York: D. Appleton-Century, 1945); M. Dufrenne, *La Personalité de base* (Paris: P.U.F., 1953). Cf. A. Kardiner, "The Concept of Basic Personality as an Operating Tool in the Social Sciences," in R. Linton, *The Science of Man in the World Crisis* (New York: Columbia University Press, 1945).

ever and however he appears, with a sympathetic effort to understand his world and his meanings. Such a method must dispense with any objective assumptions and frames. It must be ready to understand the individual as he exists in and for himself in his world which is unframed. This method has now proved its fruitfulness not only in philosophy and in social science but in psychiatry as well.[10]

It has revealed a personal freedom that is socially conditioned, not unlimited. In this respect Sartre is quite wrong. Freedom is always negatively limited by institutions and by the given situation of history. Once in existence, however, it cannot be externally caused or placed without distortion in any objective frame. The existing person activates himself spontaneously and is free to interpret the objects and institutions into which he has been thrown, and in this sense to organize a whole world of his own. This does not belong to the social world as one of its parts, for then it would be in a frame. It is a world in and for itself. The social world is only a set of conditions that exist objectively and relatively for another. In so far as it is completed, it becomes not merely a set of shared conditions but a set of free persons existing with one another and free to communicate. Each personal world is not closed but open to transcendence, and not surrounded by any objective frame. This world has a distinctive structure which is neither exclusively objective nor exclusively subjective but both together in one.

It requires a certain open discipline that can neither be objectively understood nor externally imposed, but only expressed in the actual exercise of freedom. This discipline has nothing to do with self-realization and the legal prescriptions of traditional ethics. If we wish to call it an "ethics," we must broaden this term, and even then we must think of it as an "ethics" of a most peculiar kind, belonging to an-

[10] Cf. May, *op. cit.*

other world. As we have already suggested, it departs from all the basic categories of systematic ethics. Instead of good and evil, we find choice or the failure to choose. Instead of right and wrong, we find personal integrity and disintegration. Instead of obligation, we find love; instead of justification, understatement and humility; instead of justice, forgiveness; and instead of self-realization, generosity and sacrifice.

It is not that the former terms of these pairs have no application. They apply to human beings regarded as objects, and to the behavior of human groups. They have real validity within an objective frame. The latter terms apply to the free world of the existing person. The one is an ethics of objective group behavior; the other is an ethics of subjective freedom. Neither one can exist without the other. Apart from realization, freedom cannot even exist. But apart from freedom, self-realization becomes a dead repetition of lofty principles that reeks of righteousness. In fact, without a few grains of love and mercy, the objective order of justice cannot even be effectively maintained. These existential categories, as we may call them for want of a better word, are not the special property of theologians or of any world religion. They are found the world over, wherever free persons are found.

But it may be said that this is merely an idealistic dream, the dream, perhaps, of a Christian philosopher, projecting his wishes into what he calls reality. The point that has kept the theory of a natural law alive through the ages is the fact of its so-called sanctions. Oppression and tyranny, for example, are actually followed (or punished) by resistance and rebellion. Are there any sanctions for what we have called the exercise of personal freedom? We have suggested that any human society must be finally judged by its support of personal existence.

Is it sufficiently flexible and open to encourage the exer-

cise of human freedom? Does it favor authentic human existence? Does it enable different individuals to find themselves,
each in his own way? These are the questions we must address to any human society, if we are to judge it adequately.
No matter how stable and powerful it may be, if it fails to
support these personal values, it is evil and inhuman. If it
favors them, it is good. The ruthless use of power with no
reference to these values, simply to gain an advantage over
an enemy, is wrong. The use of power for the sake of freedom can be right. If these judgments are more than private
opinions, and based on an order transcending man, we
should be able to find that violations of it are punished by
certain sanctions. Are there such sanctions?

The answer is yes! A society that uses power tyrannically,
with no respect for freedom and the values of personal existence, not only eliminates these values in the enemies it destroys but stifles them in itself. A clear example of this is the
case of Assyria, which devoted all its energies to military
conquest, neglecting the education of its citizens, as well as
all other cultural values. As a result of this, its life became
rigid and stereotyped, permitting of no creative expression
in religion, art, and science. Even its language lost its own
life, and had already been diluted and dissolved by foreign
intrusions when, in 610 B.C., it was overwhelmed by an internal insurrection and passed away almost without a trace.[11]

This sanction has been constantly at work and can be observed throughout the whole course of human history. It is
expressed in the law of institutional decline to which we
have already referred. As soon as original ideas are widely
accepted and institutionalized, they become oversimplified
and inflexible. Unless they are constantly renewed by the
exercise of human freedom, the whole civilization freezes

[11] Cf. A. Toynbee, *A Study of History* (New York: Oxford Press, 1947), pp.
338 ff.

into a fixed rigidity of convention which is unable to meet the challenge of new situations.

Nevertheless the ruthless and aggressive use of force has often been crowned by physical victory, and prolonged existence. This is often adduced as a clear-cut violation of the moral law with no clear sanction attached. Many moral sanctions, however, require some time for their fruition. Thus many persons who neglect principles of health in their youth do not suffer immediately, and pride themselves on having escaped all sanctions. Nevertheless they may suffer in the end, and may deeply affect others closely associated with them. These principles must be borne in mind in connection with any serious reflection on the nature of moral sanctions in history. These sanctions work very roughly, and require long periods of time to come to their effect. Thus the tendency to use weapons of force for political purposes has led to a constant search for more powerful weapons, which have constantly advanced in destructive power.

Until the present age of intensive scientific research, human ingenuity was able to devise instruments of only minor magnitude. Hence the notion of destruction was not yet fully developed, and its sanction remained invisible. Now, however, the idea of destruction has finally matured, and science has put in our hands really formidable weapons of great destructive power. At the same time, the necessary sanction has become quite evident. Those who employ thermonuclear weapons against their enemies will destroy themselves, or, as the moral law is expressed in the New Testament: "all they that take the sword shall perish with the sword" (Mat. 26:52). As expressed in secular language, this means that war has become futile and the traditional concept of military victory outmoded. But if we ask why this is so, and press the question, we may be able to see that this is only another way of saying that brute force, used for the national interest, is in violation of an independent order transcending man, carrying with it a necessary sanction.

4. *Christian Faith and the World of Today*

We began these chapters with an account of the global pattern of prehistoric, mythical society, and of its breakdown in ancient Greece. This breakdown released two forces, the free individual capable of making history through his choices, and the shared, rational consciousness which can master subhuman nature and lead the group to self-realization. At the beginning of our history, these forces worked together, and during other later periods, such as Hellenistic Rome and the time of the Renaissance, they achieved an unstable and precarious balance in which reason usually predominated. In our time, however, the two have fallen apart, and their essential incommensurability has clearly come to light. The individual is no longer able to understand himself and the world in which he lives by the methods of science and objective reason. Science, on the other hand, has been unable to master the human person by those objective methods which have worked so well with other objects. This opposition is, I believe, a basic factor in the crisis of our time.

In this whole history we can now see that reason on the whole has triumphed and that personal freedom has declined. This has become peculiarly evident in the modern period with the sensational advances of science and large-scale technology, the most impressive, and perhaps the final expression of the gnostic enterprise. Every accessible phase of nature and man has been subjected to objective scrutiny and analysis. Calculative methods have been refined to the last degree of perfection, and vast powers have been accumulated. This movement has been attended by the elaboration of large-scale social institutions built up to realize every human urge. The strongest and most elaborate of these is the present-day nation-state, the dominant political organization of our day.

Guiding public opinion into concerted policies by the use of mass media of communication, it calculates and organizes for the satisfaction of every objective need. Thus it watches out for public defense by the construction of weapons of mass destruction, and for the education, material welfare, and even for the amusement of its citizens by bureaus and agencies of every kind. It is futile to criticize this organization for mass welfare. It has certainly come to stay. Our very existence now depends upon it. Nevertheless we cannot fail to note the widespread *malaise* and disillusionment that have attended the growth of this intricate web of institutional structure.

Caught like a fly in one such structure, the individual by a wearing struggle escapes from it only to fall into another. Everything has been taken care of, everything seems to have its place, except himself and the strange, irrational world in which he lives. His questions are unanswered, and the meaning of the whole is lost. This threat of the meaninglessness of existence calls forth a feeling of anxiety which is not the fear of any specific object, or of all objects taken together, but which is directed rather toward an emptiness that pervades the whole of life. This feeling is manifested in many ways.

One unmistakable symptom of it is the unprecedented elaboration of techniques for psychotherapy, and the restoration of what is called mental health. But the clearest testimony to the fact that our rational tradition has failed to give us an adequate, global understanding of the human world is given by modern art and literature.[12] In all of these arts, we find a spirit of discontent and rebellion against tradi-

---

[12] See Barrett, *loc. cit.*

tional conceptions of cosmic order and beauty, as well as an honest expression of the emptiness now confronting man in the vast but inhuman field of objects which he has constructed, and on which science has focused his attention. In many of them we discern the significant groping for a new world not yet born where the individual person, unhampered by traditional virtues and codes, may find himself in those inconspicuous corners of life now dismissed by objective reason as fleeting, paltry, and homely.

The great gnostic enterprise has broken down in its time of triumph. We stand at the end of an era. We cannot go back to the age of myth. Where then are we to find a new beginning? We must turn to the past, for this is all we have. Is there a hidden source in our tradition which we may open up for a new way of life and understanding? Is there one which is relevant to the broken world in which we live? I have suggested that what we call Christianity may be such a source, and there is already cogent evidence for this suggestion.

We are all now aware of the new existential and phenomenological thought which has radically broken with the gnostic tradition and, in turning to the world of lived experience, has already brought into a clearer light those preobjective, prerational roots of human life which modern art and modern psychiatry are approaching each in its own way. It is not so commonly recognized that this new approach to human existence in the world comes to us, through the Danish thinker Kierkegaard, from the Bible. The basic existential themes are to be found in the New Testament.

The Biblical literature is not written in the artificial language of objective reason, but in the living language of the *Lebenswelt*. In fact, the world of which it so often speaks is not the cosmic order of Greek philosophy nor the factual universe of modern science, but precisely the concrete world of everyday experience. This literature is concerned with

the individual person, not as he is observed from the outside, but as he exists from within. Christian faith is deeply
and primarily concerned with this lived existence and has
developed a set of symbols like sin, grace, and faith itself
which, when understood concretely, penetrate to its very
core. It is not only aware of the mystery which is concretely
sensed in the *Lebenswelt,* but is focused upon a revealing of
this mystery which centered in concrete, historical events.
It knows of the lostness of man in his own constructions and
the emptiness of anxiety. Using concrete symbols, of which
we have spoken, and which cannot be objectively defined, it
calls upon the individual to make a decision.

This decision involves a radical break with the self-centered mode of existence that is said to lead to death, and a
resurrection from this living death into a new mode of life
no longer concerned with calculation and self-realization but
with faith, forgiveness, and sacrifice. This way of life, if lived
authentically, must transcend not only the established patterns of thought to which we are prone, but the established
moral patterns of action as well. Instead of being governed
by calculation for some form of self-realization, it must be
governed by faith and forgiveness in self-sacrifice. This mode
of existence breaks so radically with objectively oriented
customs and habits that it is referred to throughout the New
Testament as a scandal. It is this mode of Christian faith and
insight that has undergone a revival in our time, penetrating
far beyond the limits of religious institutions into secular
thought and life.

But in our Western history, this existential core of Christianity, as we may call it, which is directed to the human
person in terms of a concrete, historic revelation in the
Lebenswelt, has been rationally interpreted and objectified.
Mythical and historical content has been translated into
timeless doctrine, and faith itself rationalized into a set of
propositions about some object. Grace is held to have been

placed within the keeping of an organized institution rather than granted to the lost and wandering sheep. The free individual has no world of his own; he is either enmeshed in the order of nature or held by Grace, which is also interpreted as an "order" rather than as a way of existing. The ethic of love and sacrifice becomes a kind of self-realization.

God is regarded as an object whose major attributes can be demonstrated, and whose modes of operation analyzed and calculated, though such techniques, when applied to a sane human friend, are degrading and insulting. He is analyzed in terms of such rational categories as understanding and substance; understanding, in fact, is said to be his substance.[13] In the light of modern criticism, we can hardly fail to see the human character of this construction. It was of this that Nietzsche was thinking when he cried out in the last century that God is dead. In view of these rationalistic accretions, it is not surprising that many existential thinkers wish to sunder all connections with their religious roots, and the movement is now divided into a secular and a religious wing.

We can summarize the present situation by saying that the former is strong in its account of personal existence and freedom, but weak in its treatment of transcendence and social philosophy, while the latter is strong in these fields, but weaker in its account of the world of free existence. They make similar criticisms of the rational tradition whose weaknesses they both try to overcome by the use of the same pheonomenological method in a disciplined exploration of the concrete *Lebenswelt* of man, so long neglected by philosophy. This exploration has led them to make a similar diagnosis of the *malaise* of our cultural situation, which points to certain specific, political needs. So far, we have been concerned exclusively with ideas. It is now time for us, in conclusion, to point to the program for social action which

[13] Cf. Aquinas. *Summa Theologiae* 1.q.v.14.art.4.

these ideas suggest. How will an existential thinker look at politics at the present time?

He will regard the moral law as directed not toward order as its final end, but rather toward the free existence of the individual person in his *Lebenswelt*. The main aim that he will hold in mind is to disengage this world from the web of institutional forces that restrict and stifle it. He will recognize personal freedom as operating in an unlimited world horizon of its own. Hence he will not be interested in legislating to it. He also knows that it cannot be manipulated and contrived. Institutional structures, however, may be loosened up and opened to it, and this will underlie all his political concerns. Of every public policy he will ask: Does it prepare for, or does it actually thwart the disciplined exercise of personal freedom? From this point of view he will probably be led to conclusions of the following kind.

He will distrust the sovereign nation-state as an enormity which has now outlived its usefulness. Its mass propaganda for exclusive loyalties to itself, and the vast powers it uses to promote its own interests as against those of other states, he will regard not only as a restriction on personal freedom but as a threat to its very existence. Hence he will favor a radical separation and dilution of its vast powers. The idea of separating the nation, with its legitimate appeal for patriotism, from the administrative power of the state will appeal to him. Preserve the loyalties of small national groups to their common language and traditions. But do not let this ever coincide with sovereign, administrative power. To some extent, such a separation has been achieved in the United States, where strong local loyalties have been preserved within an administrative federal union. Such federations should always be encouraged, with a view toward building up the germinal world community now being born, and enabling it to take over those administrative powers whose exercise is essential to our survival. Everything, of course, should be done as soon as possible to strengthen the United Nations, in its struggle to administer international affairs.

The sovereignty of the nation-state will have to be abandoned if we are to survive. But there is no reason why the welfare functions of the so-called welfare state should not be administered by national groups or federations. These services, as outlined in the United Nations Declaration of Human Rights, should everywhere be centralized and strengthened as rapidly as possible, for they are required by the moral law as necessary conditions for the exercise of human freedom. As the ratio of leisure to working time increases, everything possible should be done to encourage creative hobbies, and small, primary groups where personal communication is possible. To meet this situation, a new orientation in education is essential. Aside from the professional classes, the subservient and routine jobs now available for most people no longer offer them any adequate chance for a lifetime vocation. Hence education should no longer be conceived as education for work, but rather for leisure time (or free time as it should be called) for the exercise of personal freedom. Such education will have to be much wider in scope, longer in duration, and far more arduous than what we have at present.

The study of science is, of course, essential. But every student must be given an opportunity to learn something of the life-world in which he lives and of its existential structures. This is a joint task which will require the full cooperation of history, the sciences of man, and philosophy. He should gain a sense of the wide range of choices that are open to him, and should be encouraged to make reflective choices of his own. He should also learn that freedom is lost when it becomes closed and relative to a given individual or group. It can be maintained only by an openness for communication and reinterpretation which requires severe self-discipline.

Such is the political program to which the new philosophy now points. We have examined the novel view of man on which it is based, and especially the view of social man and the moral law which is implicit within it. We have seen that it has arisen from Christian sources. Whether or not it will remain in any sense Christian, is an open question. The answer will depend on the openness of the Churches for further interpretation and development. A new sense of the world of free existence that lies between nature and Grace, between reason and faith must be regained. A new understanding of the so-called natural law must be achieved. New insights into the social world and the wider world of the individual must be revived and created. Social organization is a condition for life, not life itself in its full richness and integrity.

The Church must maintain its liturgy and its organic unity intact throughout the ages as a basis for the Christian world. But this basis is not the world itself. She must think far more seriously about the lost and wandering sheep who alone can bring this world to life by the exercise of a sacrificial freedom.

Index

Under certain headings below, page references of special importance have been given first and are separated from those which follow by a colon (e. g., Intentionality, 169-170: 133).